MW01007909

180 Days of WRITING for Kindergarten

- Prewriting
- Drafting
- Revising
- Editing
- Publishing

Author

Tracy Pearce

Shell Education

Standards

For information on how this resource meets national and other state standards, see pages 4–6. You may also review this information by scanning the QR code or visiting our website at http://www.shelleducation.com and following the on-screen directions.

Publishing Credits

Corinne Burton, M.A.Ed., *President*; Emily R. Smith, M.A.Ed., *Content Director*; Jennifer Wilson, *Editor*; Grace Alba Le, *Multimedia Designer*; Don Tran, *Production Artist*; Stephanie Bernard, *Assistant Editor*; Amber Goff, *Editorial Assistant*

Image Credits

pp. 17, 21, 33, 66, 68, 78, 99, 136, 143, 195, 197, 210, 213, iStock; All other images Shutterstock.

Standards

Shell Education

5482 Argosy Avenue
Huntington Beach, CA 92649-1030
www.tcmpub.com/shell-education
ISBN 978-1-4258-1523-3
© 2020 Shell Education Publishing, Inc.

TABLE OF CONTENTS

INTRODUCTION

The Need for Practice

To be successful in today's writing classrooms, students must deeply understand both concepts and procedures so that they can discuss and demonstrate their understanding. Demonstrating understanding is a process that must be continually practiced for students to be successful. Practice is especially important to help students apply their concrete, conceptual understanding of each particular writing skill.

Understanding Assessment

In addition to providing opportunities for frequent practice, teachers must be able to assess students' writing skills. This is important so that teachers can adequately address students' misconceptions, build on their current understandings, and challenge them appropriately. Assessment is a long-term process that involves careful analysis of student responses from a discussion, project, practice sheet, or test. When analyzing the data, it is important for teachers to reflect on how their teaching practices may have influenced students' responses and to identify those areas where additional instruction may be required. In short, the data gathered from assessments should be used to inform instruction: slow down, speed up, or reteach. This type of assessment is called *formative assessment*.

HOW TO USE THIS BOOK

With *180 Days of Writing*, creative, theme-based units guide students as they practice the five steps of the writing process: prewriting, drafting, revising, editing, and publishing. During each odd week (Weeks 1, 3, 5, etc.), students interact with mentor texts. Then, students apply their learning by writing their own pieces during each following even week (Weeks 2, 4, 6, etc.). Many practice pages also focus on grammar/language standards to help improve students' writing.

Easy to Use and Standards Based

These daily activities reinforce grade-level skills across the various genres of writing: opinion, informative/explanatory, and narrative. Each day provides a full practice page, making the activities easy to prepare and implement as part of a classroom morning routine, at the beginning of each writing lesson, or as homework.

The chart below indicates the writing and language standards that are addressed throughout this book. See pages 5–6 for a breakdown of which writing standard is covered in each week. **Note:** Students may not have deep understandings of some topics in this book. Remember to assess students based on their writing skills and not their content knowledge.

College and Career Readiness Standards

Writing K.1—Use a combination of drawing, dictating, and writing to compose opinion pieces in which they tell a reader the topic or the name of the book they are writing about and state an opinion or preference about the topic or the book.
Writing K.2—Use a combination of drawing, dictating, and writing to compose informative/explanatory texts in which they name what they are writing about and supply some information about the topic.
Writing K.3—Use a combination of drawing, dictating, and writing to narrate a single event or several loosely linked events, tell about the events in the order in which they occurred, and provide a reaction to what happened.
Language K.1—Demonstrate command of the conventions of standard English grammar and usage when writing or speaking.
Language K.2—Demonstrate command of the conventions of standard English capitalization, punctuation, and spelling when writing.

HOW TO USE THIS BOOK (cont.)

Below is a list of overarching themes, corresponding weekly themes, and the writing standards that students will encounter throughout this book. For each overarching theme, students will interact with mentor texts in the odd week and then apply their learning by writing their own pieces in the even week. **Note:** The writing prompt for each week can be found on pages 7–8. You may wish to display the prompts in the classroom for students to reference throughout the appropriate weeks.

Overarching Themes	Weekly Themes	Standards
Park	**Week 1:** Playing at the Park **Week 2:** Picnic at the Park	**Writing K.3**—Narrate a single event or several loosely linked events. Tell about the events in the order in which they occurred, and provide a reaction to what happened.
School	**Week 3:** What We Do in School **Week 4:** School Rules	**Writing K.3**—Narrate a single event or several loosely linked events. Tell about the events in the order in which they occurred, and provide a reaction to what happened.
Seasons	**Week 5:** Spring or Fall? **Week 6:** Summer or Winter?	**Writing K.1**—Compose opinion pieces in which they tell a reader the topic or the name of the book they are writing about and state an opinion or preference about the topic or the book.
The Five Senses	**Week 7:** Sight and Smell **Week 8:** Taste and Touch	**Writing K.2**—Compose informative/explanatory texts in which they name what they are writing about and supply some information about the topic.
Community Heroes	**Week 9:** Firefighters **Week 10:** Police Officers	**Writing K.2**—Compose informative/explanatory texts in which they name what they are writing about and supply some information about the topic.
Nursery Rhymes	**Week 11:** Humpty Dumpty or Jack and Jill? **Week 12:** Itsy Bitsy Spider or Little Bo Peep?	**Writing K.1**—Compose opinion pieces in which they tell a reader the topic or the name of the book they are writing about and state an opinion or preference about the topic or the book.
Solar System	**Week 13:** Sun and Moon **Week 14:** Earth	**Writing K.2**—Compose informative/explanatory texts in which they name what they are writing about and supply some information about the topic.
Holidays	**Week 15:** Christmas or St. Patrick's Day? **Week 16:** Valentine's Day or Halloween?	**Writing K.1**—Compose opinion pieces in which they tell a reader the topic or the name of the book they are writing about and state an opinion or preference about the topic or the book.
Animals	**Week 17:** Ocean Animals **Week 18:** Land Animals	**Writing K.2**—Compose informative/explanatory texts in which they name what they are writing about and supply some information about the topic.

HOW TO USE THIS BOOK *(cont.)*

Overarching Themes	Weekly Themes	Standards
Nature	**Week 19:** Farms **Week 20:** Forests	**Writing K.3**—Narrate a single event or several loosely linked events. Tell about the events in the order in which they occurred, and provide a reaction to what happened.
Sports	**Week 21:** Soccer **Week 22:** Baseball	**Writing K.3**—Narrate a single event or several loosely linked events. Tell about the events in the order in which they occurred, and provide a reaction to what happened.
People We Know	**Week 23:** Family **Week 24:** Friends	**Writing K.3**—Narrate a single event or several loosely linked events. Tell about the events in the order in which they occurred, and provide a reaction to what happened.
Pets	**Week 25:** Pet Hamsters or Bunnies? **Week 26:** Pet Dogs or Cats?	**Writing K.1**—Compose opinion pieces in which they tell a reader the topic or the name of the book they are writing about and state an opinion or preference about the topic or the book.
Birthdays	**Week 27:** My Birthday **Week 28:** Favorite Birthday Party	**Writing K.3**—Narrate a single event or several loosely linked events. Tell about the events in the order in which they occurred, and provide a reaction to what happened.
Food	**Week 29:** Apples or Oranges? **Week 30:** Ice Cream or Cookies?	**Writing K.1**—Compose opinion pieces in which they tell a reader the topic or the name of the book they are writing about and state an opinion or preference about the topic or the book.
Birds	**Week 31:** Peacocks **Week 32:** Ducks	**Writing K.2**—Compose informative/explanatory texts in which they name what they are writing about and supply some information about the topic.
Weather	**Week 33:** Hot or Cold? **Week 34:** Wind or Rain?	**Writing K.1**—Compose opinion pieces in which they tell a reader the topic or the name of the book they are writing about and state an opinion or preference about the topic or the book.
How To . . .	**Week 35:** How to Make a Peanut Butter and Jelly Sandwich **Week 36:** How to Wash Your Hands	**Writing K.2**—Compose informative/explanatory texts in which they name what they are writing about and supply some information about the topic.

HOW TO USE THIS BOOK (cont.)

Weekly Setup

Write each prompt on the board throughout the appropriate week. Students should reference the prompts as they work through the activity pages so that they stay focused on the topics and the right genre of writing: opinion, informative/explanatory, and narrative. You may wish to print copies of this chart from the digital resources (filename: GK_writingprompts.pdf) and distribute them to students to keep throughout the school year.

Week	Prompt
1	Write about a time you played at the park.
2	Write about a time you had a picnic.
3	Write about what you do at school.
4	Write about a school rule that you follow.
5	Write about spring or fall.
6	Write about summer or winter.
7	Write about something you see or smell.
8	Write about something you taste or touch.
9	Write about firefighters. Tell what they do.
10	Write about police officers. Tell what they do.

Week	Prompt
11	Write about *Humpty Dumpty* or *Jack and Jill*.
12	Write about *The Itsy Bitsy Spider* or *Little Bo Peep*.
13	Write about the sun or the moon.
14	Write about Earth.
15	Write about Christmas or St. Patrick's Day.
16	Write about Valentine's Day or Halloween.
17	Write about ocean animals.
18	Write about land animals.
19	Write about spending time on a farm.
20	Write about spending time in a forest.
21	Write about a soccer game.

HOW TO USE THIS BOOK *(cont.)*

Week	Prompt
22	Write about a baseball game.
23	Write about spending a day with your family.
24	Write about spending a day with a friend.
25	Write about a hamster or a bunny.
26	Write about a dog or a cat.
27	Write about a birthday party you have had.
28	Write about your favorite birthday party.
29	Write about apples or oranges.
30	Write about ice cream or cookies.
31	Write about peacocks.

Week	Prompt
32	Write about ducks.
33	Write about hot or cold weather.
34	Write about wind or rain.
35	Write about making a peanut butter and jelly sandwich.
36	Write about washing your hands.

#51523—180 Days of Writing

HOW TO USE THIS BOOK (cont.)

Using the Practice Pages

The activity pages provide practice and assessment opportunities for each day of the school year. For this age level, teachers may wish to complete the pages together as a class. Teachers may wish to prepare packets of weekly practice pages for the classroom or for homework. As outlined on pages 5–6, each two-week unit is aligned to one writing standard. **Note:** Before implementing each week's activity pages, review the corresponding prompt on pages 7–8 with students and have students brainstorm thoughts about each topic.

On odd weeks, students practice the daily skills using mentor texts. On even weeks, students use what they have learned in the previous week and apply it to their own writing.

Each day focuses on one of the steps in the writing process: prewriting, drafting, revising, editing, and publishing.

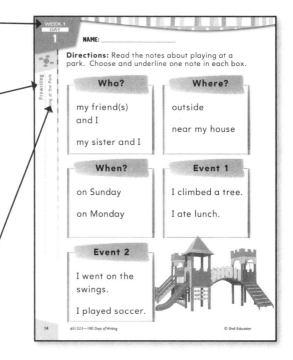

There are 18 overarching themes. Each odd week and the following even week focus on unique themes that fit under one overarching theme. For a list of the overarching themes and individual weekly themes, see pages 5–6.

Using the Resources

The following resources will be helpful to students as they complete the activity pages. Print copies of these resources and provide them to students to keep at their desks.

Rubrics for the three genres of writing (opinion, informative/explanatory, and narrative) can be found on pages 199–201. Use the rubrics to assess students' writing at the end of each even week. Be sure to share these rubrics with students often so that they know what is expected of them.

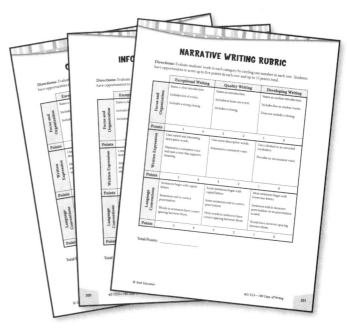

HOW TO USE THIS BOOK (cont.)

Using the Resources (cont.)

The Writing Process can be found on page 205 and in the digital resources (filename: GK_writing_process. pdf). Students can reference each step of the writing process as they move through each week.

Editing Marks can be found on page 206 and in the digital resources (filename: GK_ editing_marks.pdf). Students may need to reference this page as they work on the editing activities (Day 4s).

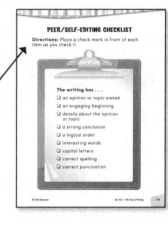

If you wish to have students peer or self-edit their writing, a *Peer/Self-Editing Checklist* is provided on page 213 and in the digital resources (filename: peer_ checklist.pdf).

Writing Signs for each of the writing genres are on pages 210–212 and in the digital resources (filename: GK_writing_signs.pdf). Hang the signs up during the appropriate two-week units to remind students which type of writing they are focusing on.

Writing Tips for each of the writing genres can be found on pages 207–209 and in the digital resources (filename: GK_writing_tips.pdf). Students can reference the appropriate *Writing Tips* pages as they work through the weeks.

HOW TO USE THIS BOOK (cont.)

Diagnostic Assessment

Teachers can use the practice pages as diagnostic assessments. The data analysis tools included with the book enable teachers or parents to quickly score students' work and monitor their progress. Teachers and parents can quickly see which writing skills students may need to target further to develop proficiency.

After students complete each two-week unit, score each students' even week Day 5 published piece using the appropriate, genre-specific rubric (pages 199–201). Then, complete the *Practice Page Item Analysis* (pages 202–204) that matches the writing genre. These charts are also provided in the digital resources (filenames: GK_opinion_analysis.pdf, GK_inform_analysis.pdf, GK_narrative_analysis.pdf). Teachers can input data into the electronic files directly on the computer, or they can print the pages and analyze students' work using paper and pencil.

To Complete the Practice Page Item Analyses:

- Write or type students' names in the far-left column. Depending on the number of students, more than one copy of the form may be needed or you may need to add rows.

- The weeks in which the particular writing genres are the focus are indicated across the tops of the charts. **Note:** Students are only assessed on the even weeks, therefore the odd weeks are not included on the charts.

- For each student, record his or her rubric score in the appropriate column.

- Add the scores for each student after they've focused on a particular writing genre twice. Place that sum in the far right column. Use these scores as benchmarks to determine how each student is performing. This allows for three benchmarks during the year that you can use to gather formative diagnostic data.

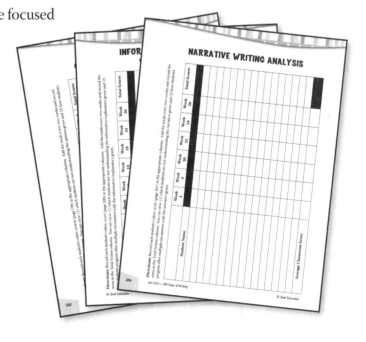

HOW TO USE THIS BOOK *(cont.)*

Using the Results to Differentiate Instruction

Once results are gathered and analyzed, teachers can use the results to inform the way they differentiate instruction. The data can help determine which writing types are the most difficult for students and which students need additional instructional support and continued practice.

Whole-Class Support

The results of the diagnostic analysis may show that the entire class is struggling with a particular writing genre. If these concepts have been taught in the past, this indicates that further instruction or reteaching is necessary. If these concepts have not been taught in the past, this data is a great preassessment and may demonstrate that students do not have a working knowledge of the concepts. Thus, careful planning for the length of the unit(s) or lesson(s) must be considered, and additional front-loading may be required.

Small-Group or Individual Support

The results of the diagnostic analysis may show that an individual student or a small group of students is struggling with a particular writing genre. If these concepts have been taught in the past, this indicates that further instruction or reteaching is necessary. Consider pulling these students aside to instruct them further on the concept(s), while others are working independently. Students may also benefit from extra practice using games or computer-based resources. Teachers can also use the results to help identify individual students or groups of proficient students who are ready for enrichment or above-grade-level instruction. These students may benefit from independent learning contracts or more challenging activities.

Digital Resources

Reference page 214 for information about accessing the digital resources and an overview of the contents.

STANDARDS CORRELATIONS

Shell Education is committed to producing educational materials that are research and standards based. In this effort, we have correlated all of our products to the academic standards of all 50 states, the District of Columbia, the Department of Defense Dependents Schools, and all Canadian provinces.

How to Find Standards Correlations

To print a customized correlation report of this product for your state, visit our website at **www.tcmpub.com/shell-education** and follow the on-screen directions. If you require assistance in printing correlation reports, please contact our Customer Service Department at 1-877-777-3450.

Purpose and Intent of Standards

Legislation mandates that all states adopt academic standards that identify the skills students will learn in kindergarten through grade twelve. Many states also have standards for Pre-K. This same legislation sets requirements to ensure the standards are detailed and comprehensive.

Standards are designed to focus instruction and guide adoption of curricula. Standards are statements that describe the criteria necessary for students to meet specific academic goals. They define the knowledge, skills, and content students should acquire at each level. Standards are also used to develop standardized tests to evaluate students' academic progress.

Teachers are required to demonstrate how their lessons meet state standards. State standards are used in the development of all of our products, so educators can be assured they meet the academic requirements of each state.

The activities in this book are aligned to today's national and state-specific college and career readiness standards. The chart on page 4 lists the writing and language standards used throughout this book. A more detailed chart on pages 5–6 correlates the specific writing standards to each week.

NAME: _____

Directions: Read the notes about playing at a park. Choose and underline one note in each box.

Who?

my friend(s)
and I

my sister and I

Where?

outside

near my house

When?

on Sunday

on Monday

Event 1

I climbed a tree.

I ate lunch.

Event 2

I went on the swings.

I played soccer.

NAME: _____

Directions: Read the text. Then, underline each sentence in green, red, or blue.

Green: introduction   **Red:** event   **Blue:** closure

I went to the park on Sunday with my sister. First, we played on the swings. Then, we went down the slide. We had a great day.

Printing Practice

Directions: Trace the *Pp*'s. Write your own.

Revising

Playing at the Park

NAME: _____

Directions: Look at the picture. Circle the details.

Directions: Draw your favorite detail from the picture.

NAME: _____

Directions: Look for periods. Circle the correct sentences.

Example: (Pat rides on the swings.)
Pat rides on the swings

1. Al goes down the slide

   Al goes down the slide.

2. Liz plays in the sand.

   Liz plays in the sand

3. She runs to the swings.

   She runs to the swings

4. I am on the seesaw

   I am on the seesaw.

NAME: _____

Directions: Read the text. Draw a picture. Fill in the checklist.

> I went to the park on Sunday with my sister. First, we played on the swings. Then, we went down the slide. We had a great day.

Checklist ☑

❑ Sentences begin with capital letters.

❑ Sentences end with punctuation.

❑ There are spaces between the words.

NAME: _____

Directions: Think about a picnic at the park. Draw notes about the day.

Who?

Where?

When?

Event 1

Event 2

NAME: _____

Drafting

Picnic at the Park

Directions: Write about a picnic. Fill in the checklist.

Introduction

I had a picnic with _____

_ _

_____.

Events

_____

First, _____.

Then, _____.

Closing Sentence

_____

_ _

_____

and I had so much fun!

Checklist ☑

❑ I have an introduction.

❑ I have events.

❑ I have a closing.

NAME: _____

Directions: Add details to the picture.

NAME: _____

Directions: Add periods to the sentences.

Example: Jim is flying a kite_.

1. Nic sits on a blanket

2. She eats a roll

3. I look in the basket

4. The park is fun

NAME: _____

Directions: Draw and write about a picnic. Fill in the checklist.

_____

- -

_____

- -

_____

- -

_____

Checklist ✔

❑ Sentences begin with capital letters.

❑ Sentences end with punctuation.

❑ There are spaces between words.

NAME: _____

Directions: Read the notes about a day at school. Choose and underline one note in each box.

Who?

my classmates and I

my teacher and I

Where?

on the playground

in the classroom

When?

today

yesterday

Event 1

I practiced math.

I played on the monkey bars.

Event 2

I went down the slide.

I drew a picture.

NAME: _____

Directions: Read the text. Then, underline each sentence in green, red, or blue.

Green: introduction   **Red:** event   **Blue:** closure

Today, I went to school. First, we did school work. Then, we went to recess. I had a lot of fun at school.

$$1 + 2 = 3$$

Printing Practice abc

Directions: Trace the *Ll*'s. Write your own.

L L L

NAME: _____

Directions: Look at the picture. Circle the details.

Directions: Draw your favorite detail from the picture.

#51523—180 Days of Writing

NAME: _____

Directions: Look for spacing. Circle the correct sentences.

Example: Jim plays with blocks.
Jimplays with blocks.

1. I read a story.

   Iread a story.

2. Heeats lunch.

   He eats lunch.

3. Luz playsat recess.

   Luz plays at recess.

4. We do a puzzle.

   Wedo a puzzle.

NAME: _____

Directions: Read the text. Draw a picture. Fill in the checklist.

Today, I went to school. First, we did school work. Then, we went to recess. I had a lot of fun at school.

Checklist ☑

❑ Sentences begin with capital letters.

❑ Sentences end with punctuation.

❑ There are spaces between the words.

#51523—180 Days of Writing   © Shell Education

NAME: _____

Directions: Think about a school rule that you follow. Draw notes about it.

Who?

Where?

When?

Event 1

Event 2

NAME: _____

Directions: Write about a school rule. Fill in the checklist.

Introduction

I followed a rule with
_____
- - - - - - - - - - - - - - - - -
_____ .

Events _____
- - - - - - - - - - - - - - - - -
First, _____ .
_____
- - - - - - - - - - - - - - - - -
Then, _____ .

Closing Sentence
_____
- - - - - - - - - - - - - - - - -
_____

and I follow rules.

Checklist ☑

❏ I have an introduction.

❏ I have events.

❏ I have a closing.

NAME: _____

Directions: Add details to the picture.

Editing
School Rules

NAME: _____

Directions: Look for spacing. Complete the sentences.

Example: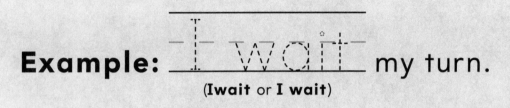

I wait my turn.
(**Iwait** or **I wait**)

1. Zan raises _____.

   (**his hand** or **hishand**)

2. _____ a good listener.

   (**Heis** or **He is**)

3. She shares _____.

   (**her toys** or **hertoys**)

NAME: _____

Directions: Draw and write about a school rule. Fill in the checklist.

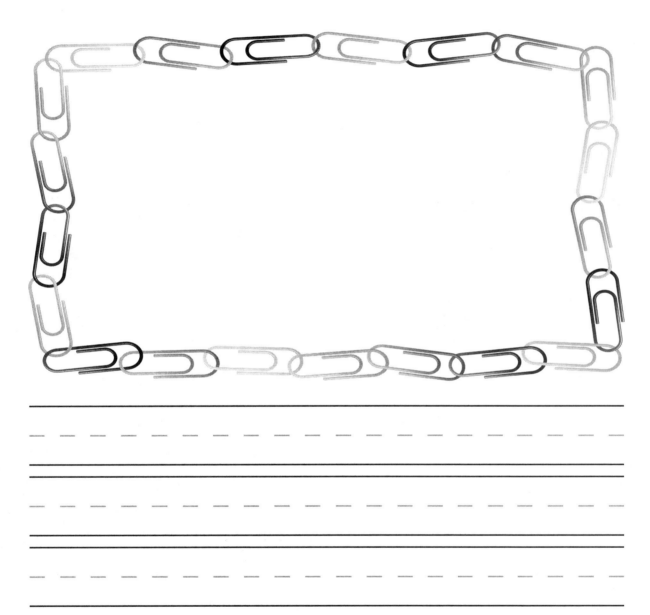

_____

- - - - - - - - - - - - - - - - - - - -

_____

- - - - - - - - - - - - - - - - - - - -

_____

- - - - - - - - - - - - - - - - - - - -

_____

Checklist ☑

❑ Sentences begin with capital letters.

❑ Sentences end with punctuation.

❑ There are spaces between words.

Prewriting
Spring or Fall?

NAME: _____

Directions: Circle the picture you like best.

Opinion: I like . . .

spring

fall

Directions: Place a check mark next to a reason.

Reasons

_____ I like leaves.   _____ I like sunshine.

_____ I like flowers.   _____ I like clouds.

NAME: _____

Directions: Read the text. Then, underline each sentence in green, red or blue.

Green:
opinion

Red:
detail

Blue:
closure

I like spring more than fall. I like it because there are lots of fun things I can do. Spring is the best season.

Printing Practice

Directions: Trace the *Ss*'s. Write your own.

NAME: _____

Directions: Match the sentences to the pictures.

1. He likes the pumpkin.

2. I plant flowers.

3. She bounces a ball.

4. The sun is bright.

5. I see a leaf.

NAME: _____

Directions: Look for periods. Circle the correct sentences.

Example: Leaves are falling
(Leaves are falling.)

1. It is raining.

   It is raining

2. Here is a pumpkin.

   Here is a pumpkin

3. The flower is pink

   The flower is pink.

4. I like the rain.

   I like the rain

Publishing
Spring or Fall?

NAME: _____

Directions: Read the text. Draw a picture. Fill in the checklist.

I like spring more than fall. I like it because there are lots of fun things I can do. Spring is the best season.

Checklist ☑

❑ Sentences begin with capital letters.

❑ Sentences end with punctuation.

❑ There are spaces between the words.

NAME: _____

Directions: Circle the picture you like best. Write your opinion. Write a reason.

summer   winter

Opinion

I like _____.

Reason

I like it because _____

_____.

NAME: _____

Directions: Write about summer or winter. Fill in the checklist.

Opinion

_____

_____ is the best season.

(**Summer** or **Winter**)

Reason _____

I like it because _____

_____.

Closing _____

I love _____!

(**summer** or **winter**)

Checklist ☑

❏ I state my opinion.

❏ I have a detail.

❏ I have a closing.

NAME: _____

Directions: Read the sentences. Draw pictures to match.

1. They build a snowman.

2. It is hot.

3. The snow is falling.

Editing
Summer or Winter?

NAME: _____

Directions: Add periods to the sentences.

Example: It is cold_

1. I like to swim

2. The bear sleeps

3. They play in snow

4. I go to the beach

5. I wear a coat

NAME: _____

Directions: Draw and write about summer or winter. Fill in the checklist.

_____

- -

_____

_____

- -

_____

_____

- -

_____

Checklist ☑

☐ Sentences begin with capital letters.

☐ Sentences end with punctuation.

☐ There are spaces between words.

NAME: _____

Directions: Circle the pictures about sight and smell.

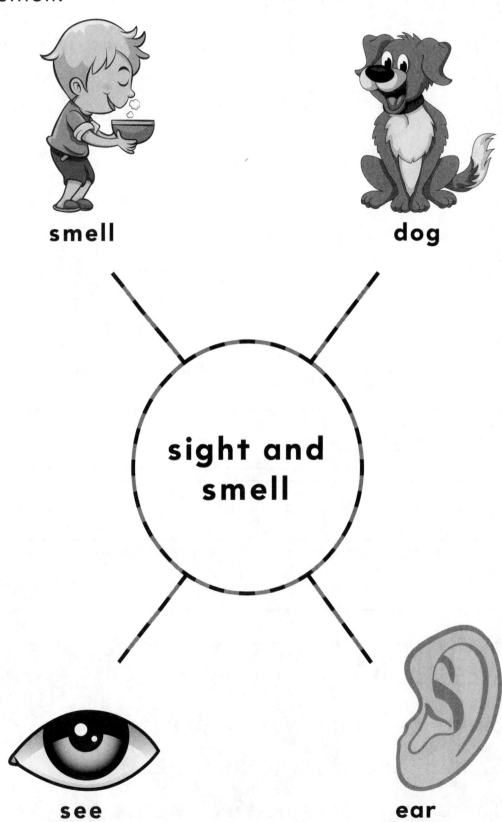

smell

dog

sight and smell

see

ear

#51523—180 Days of Writing

NAME: _____

Directions: Read the text. Then, underline each sentence in green, red, or blue.

Green: topic	**Red:** detail	**Blue:** closure

We have five senses.

We use our eyes to see.

We use our noses to smell. It is great to have senses!

Printing Practice 📝

Directions: Trace the *Ee*'s. Write your own.

E e   E e   _____

NAME: _____

Directions: Choose a word. Underline it.

Example: I (<u>smell</u> or **sniff**) my food.

1. I (**see** or **saw**) my mom.

2. I smell a (**flower** or **tree**).

3. I see a (**bird** or **butterfly**).

4. I (**like** or **love**) my senses.

NAME: _____

Directions: Look for capital letters. Circle the correct sentences.

Example: (He smells a flower.)
he smells a flower.

1. She smells pizza.

   she smells pizza.

2. i see flowers.

   I see flowers.

3. They smell muffins.

   they smell muffins.

NAME: _____

Directions: Read the text. Draw a picture. Fill in the checklist.

> We have five senses. We use our eyes to see. We use our noses to smell. It is great to have senses!

Checklist ☑

❑ Sentences begin with capital letters.

❑ Sentences end with punctuation.

❑ There are spaces between the words.

NAME: _____

Directions: Trace the words about taste and touch.

apple   bunny

taste and
touch

pencil   touch

Drafting

Taste and Touch

NAME: _____

Directions: Write about taste or touch. Fill in the checklist.

Topic

_____

I use my sense of _____.

(**taste** or **touch**)

Detail

_____

I use it to _____

- -

_____.

Closing

_____

I like to _____.

(**taste** or **touch**)

Checklist ☑

❑ I have a topic.

❑ I have a detail.

❑ I have a closing.

#51523—180 Days of Writing © *Shell Education*

NAME: _____

Directions: Choose a word. Write it.

Example: I smell a _____flower_____.
(**rose** or **flower**)

1. She tastes a _____.
(**cookie** or **candy**)

2. He feels a _____.
(**bed** or **bell**)

3. She feels a _____.
(**cat** or **dog**)

4. He eats _____.
(**pizza** or **cheese**)

NAME: _____

Directions: Choose the correct word. Write it.

Example: _____ touch the cat.

(**They** or **they**)

1. _____ taste the apple.

(**I** or **i**)

2. _____ feels the crayon.

(**he** or **He**)

3. _____ feels a horse.

(**She** or **she**)

4. _____ eat cookies.

(**I** or **i**)

 #51523—180 Days of Writing

NAME: _____

Directions: Draw and write about taste or touch. Fill in the checklist.

_____

- - - - - - - - - - - - - - - - - -

_____

_____

- - - - - - - - - - - - - - - - - -

_____

Checklist ✔

❑ Sentences begin with capital letters.

❑ Sentences end with punctuation.

❑ There are spaces between words.

Prewriting

Firefighters

NAME: _____

Directions: Circle the pictures about firefighters.

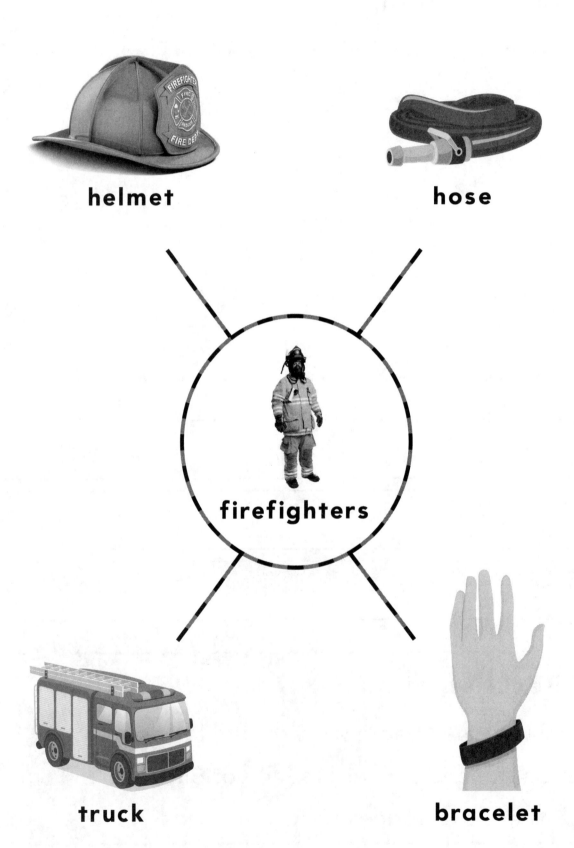

helmet

hose

firefighters

truck

bracelet

#51523—180 Days of Writing

NAME: _____

Directions: Read the text. Then, underline each sentence in green, red, or blue.

Green: topic	**Red:** detail	**Blue:** closure

Firefighters help the community. They keep people safe. They stop fires. Firefighters are heroes.

Printing Practice

Directions: Trace the *Ff*'s. Write your own.

Ff Ff _____

NAME: _____

Directions: Choose a word. Underline it.

Example: Firefighters (**can** or <u>**will**</u>) put out fires.

1. Firefighters (**rescue** or **help**) people.

2. Firefighters (**drive** or **steer**) trucks.

3. Firefighters (**use** or **carry**) ladders.

4. Firefighters (**wear** or **have**) jackets.

NAME: _____

Directions: Look for periods. Circle the correct sentences.

Example: Firefighters have boots
(Firefighters have boots.)

1. Firefighters rescue people

   Firefighters rescue people.

2. Firefighters use ladders.

   Firefighters use ladders

3. Firefighters work at fire stations.

   Firefighters work at fire stations

NAME: _____

Directions: Read the text. Draw a picture. Fill in the checklist.

Firefighters help the community. They keep people safe. They stop fires. Firefighters are heroes.

Checklist ☑

❑ Sentences begin with capital letters.

❑ Sentences end with punctuation.

❑ There are spaces between the words.

NAME: _____

Directions: Trace the words about police officers.

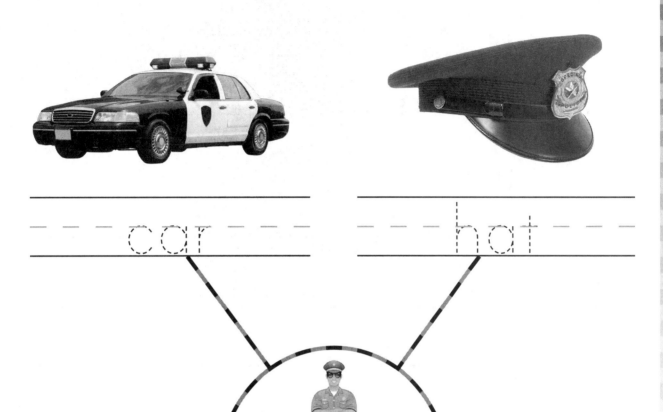

car   hat

police
officers

lollipop   badge

Drafting
Police Officers

NAME: _____

Directions: Write about police officers. Fill in the checklist.

Topic

Police officers _____ people.
(**save** or **help**)

Detail

They _____
_____
_____.

Closing

Police officers are _____.
(**kind** or **brave**)

Checklist ☑

❏ I have a topic sentence.

❏ I have a detail.

❏ I have a closing.

 #51523—180 Days of Writing

Revising

Police Officers

NAME: _____

Directions: Choose a word. Write it.

Example: Police officers work ___in___ police stations.
(**at** or **in**)

1. Police officers keep _____ safe.
(**me** or **us**)

2. Police officers _____ tickets.
(**give** or **have**)

3. Police officers _____ laws.
(**obey** or **follow**)

4. Police officers are _____.
(**kind** or **brave**)

Editing

Police Officers

NAME: _____

Directions: Add periods to the sentences.

Example: Police officers help people.

1. Police officers wear badges

2. They drive in cars with sirens

3. Police officers wear uniforms

4. Police officers work very hard

5. Police officers are heroes

 #51523—180 Days of Writing

NAME: _____

Directions: Draw and write about police officers. Fill in the checklist.

Checklist ☑

❑ Sentences begin with capital letters.

❑ Sentences end with punctuation.

❑ There are spaces between words.

NAME: _____

Directions: Circle the picture you like best.

Opinion: I like . . .

Humpty Dumpty   **Jack and Jill**

Directions: Place a check mark next to a reason.

Reasons

____ They are nice.   ____ He is funny.

____ He falls off   ____ They fall down
     a wall.   a hill.

NAME: _____

Directions: Read the text. Then, underline each sentence in green, red, or blue.

Green:	**Red:**	**Blue:**
opinion	detail	closure

I like "Jack and Jill" more than "Humpty Dumpty." I like it because it is funny. "Jack and Jill" is my favorite.

Printing Practice

Directions: Trace the *Jj*'s. Write your own.

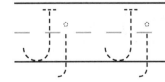

Revising

Humpty Dumpty or Jack and Jill?

NAME: _____

Directions: Match the sentences to the pictures.

1. Jack fell down.

2. Humpty Dumpty
   fell.

3. Jill had a pail.

4. Jack and Jill
   went up a hill.

NAME: _____

Directions: Look for spacing. Circle the
correct sentences.

Example: Jack and Jill wentup the hill.
Jack and Jill went up the hill.

1. Jack fell down.

   Jack felldown.

2. AndJill came tumbling after.

   And Jill came tumbling after.

3. Jack and Jill were both okay.

   Jackand Jill were both okay.

NAME: _____

Directions: Read the text. Draw a picture. Fill in the checklist.

I like "Jack and Jill" more than "Humpty Dumpty." I like it because it is funny. "Jack and Jill" is my favorite.

Checklist ☑

❏ Sentences begin with capital letters.

❏ Sentences end with punctuation.

❏ There are spaces between words.

NAME: _____

Directions: Circle the picture you like best. Write your opinion. Write a reason.

Itsy Bitsy Spider   **Little Bo Peep**

Opinion

_____

I like _____.

Reason

_____

I like it because _____

_____.

Drafting

Itsy Bitsy Spider or Little Bo Peep?

NAME: _____

Directions: Write about "Itsy Bitsy Spider" or "Little Bo Peep." Fill in the checklist.

Opinion

_____

_ _ _ _ _ _ _ _ _ _ _ _ _ _ _ _ _

_____

("**Itsy Bitsy Spider**" or "**Little Bo Peep**")

is the best rhyme.

Reason

_____

I like it because _____

_ _ _ _ _ _ _ _ _ _ _ _ _ _ _ _ _

_____.

Closing

_____

I love _____.

("**Itsy Bitsy Spider**" or "**Little Bo Peep**")

_____

Checklist ☑

❑ I state my opinion.

❑ I have a detail.

❑ I have a closing.

NAME: _____

Directions: Read the sentences. Draw pictures to match.

1. I see a spider.

2. There is a sheep.

3. Little Bo Peep is sad.

Editing

Itsy Bitsy Spider or Little Bo Peep?

NAME: _____

Directions: Choose the words. Write them.

Example: __She likes__ her sheep.

(**Shelikes** or **She likes**)

1. The sheep _____.

(**arelost** or **are lost**)

2. The spider climbs _____.

(**a web** or **aweb**)

3. I see _____.

(**asheep** or **a sheep**)

4. _____ the spider.

(**I see** or **Isee**)

NAME: _____

Directions: Draw and write about "Itsy Bitsy Spider" or "Little Bo Peep." Fill in the checklist.

_____

- -

_____

_____

- -

_____

_____

- -

_____

Checklist ☑

☐ Sentences begin with capital letters.

☐ Sentences end with punctuation.

☐ There are spaces between words.

Prewriting
Sun and Moon

NAME: _____

Directions: Circle the pictures about the sun or the moon.

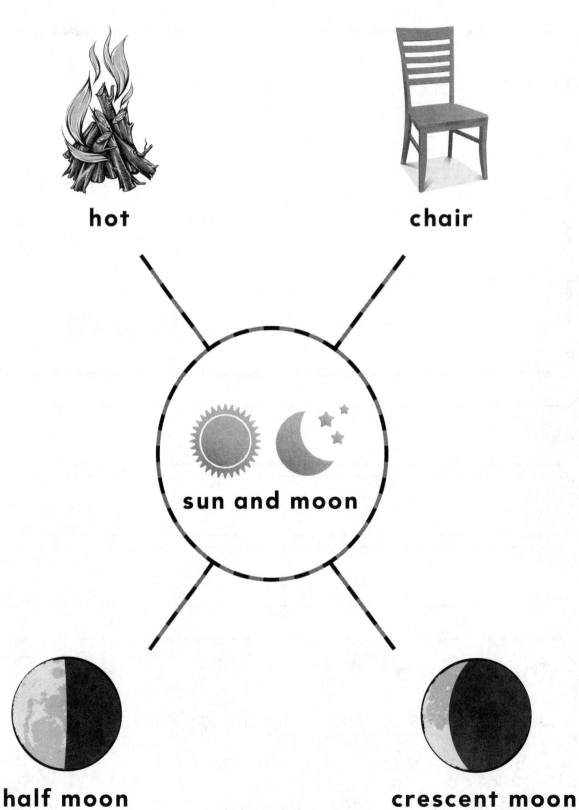

hot

chair

sun and moon

half moon

crescent moon

NAME: _____

Directions: Read the text. Then, underline each sentence in green, red, or blue.

Green:
topic

Red:
detail

Blue:
closure

The sun and the moon are in the sky. The sun comes out in the day. The moon comes out at night. They are both important to Earth.

Printing Practice _abc_

Directions: Trace the _Mm_'s. Write your own.

NAME: _____

Directions: Choose a word. Underline it.

Example: The sun and moon are (**big** or **huge**).

1. The sun is a (**big** or **huge**) star.

2. The (**sun** or **moon**) is in the sky.

3. Earth (**has** or **gets**) light from the sun.

4. We (**see** or **saw**) the moon at night.

NAME: _____

Directions: Look for capital letters. Circle the correct sentences.

> **Example:** (The sun is a big star.)
> the sun is a big star.

1. the sun is bright.

   The sun is bright.

2. The moon is smaller than Earth.

   the moon is smaller than Earth.

3. the sun is hot.

   The sun is hot.

NAME: _____

Publishing

Sun and Moon

Directions: Read the text. Draw a picture. Fill in the checklist.

The sun and the moon are in the sky. The sun comes out in the day. The moon comes out at night. They are both important to Earth.

Checklist ☑

❑ Sentences begin with capital letters.

❑ Sentences end with punctuation.

❑ There are spaces between words.

NAME: _____

Directions: Trace the words about features of Earth.

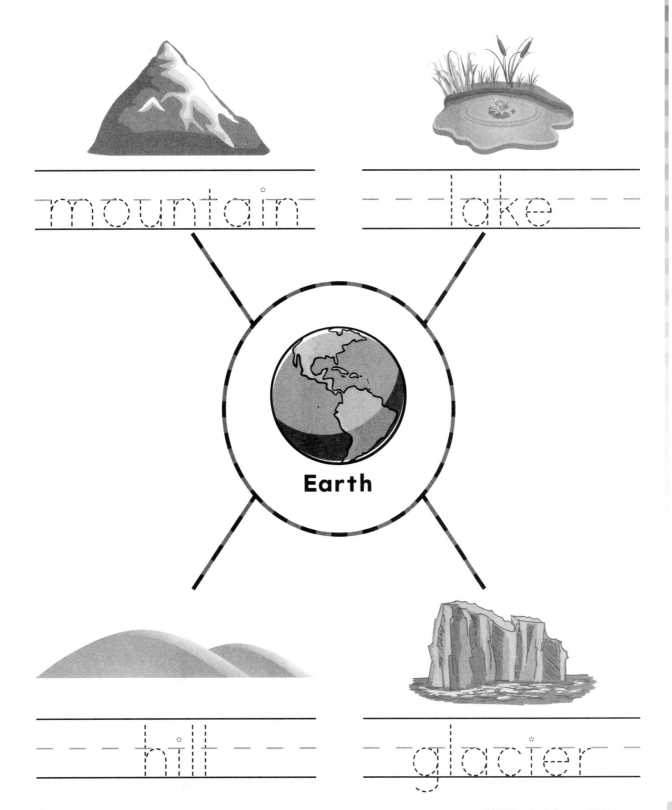

mountain

lake

Earth

hill

glacier

Drafting | Earth

NAME: _____

Directions: Write about Earth. Fill in the checklist.

Topic _____

There are _____ things

(**lots of** or **many**)

about Earth.

Detail _____

Earth has _____

_____.

Closing _____

Earth is _____.

Checklist ☑

☐ I have a topic sentence.

☐ I have a detail.

☐ I have a closing.

NAME: _____

Directions: Choose a word. Write it.

Example: There are ___eight___ planets.
(**eight** or **8**)

_____

1. Earth _____ around the sun.
   (**goes** or **travels**)

_____

2. Earth has _____ moon.
   (**1** or **one**)

_____

3. Earth is _____.
   (**large** or **big**)

_____

4. Earth _____ energy from the sun.
   (**has** or **gets**)

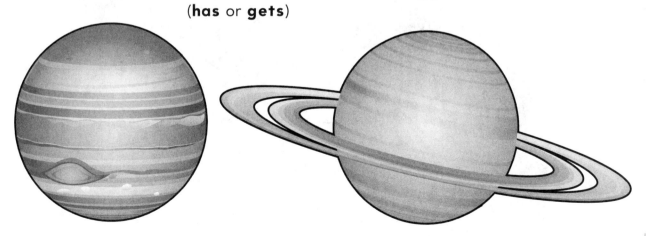

Editing | Earth

NAME: _____

Directions: Choose the correct word. Write it.

Example: _The_ planet Jupiter is big.
(**the** or **The**)

1. _____ planets go around the sun.
(**the** or **The**)

2. _____ are eight planets.
(**There** or **there**)

3. _____ planet Earth is mostly water.
(**the** or **The**)

NAME: _____

Directions: Draw and write about Earth.
Fill in the checklist.

_____

_____

_____

_____

_____

_____

Checklist ☑

❑ Sentences begin with capital letters.

❑ Sentences end with punctuation.

❑ There are spaces between words.

NAME: _____

Directions: Circle the picture you like best.

Opinion: I like . . .

Christmas	**St. Patrick's Day**

Directions: Place a check mark next to a reason.

Reasons

_____ We wear green.

_____ We decorate a tree.

_____ We open gifts.

_____ There are pots of gold.

NAME: _____

Directions: Read the text. Then, underline each sentence in green, red, or blue.

Green: opinion **Red:** detail **Blue:** closure

I like St. Patrick's Day. I like it because I get to wear green. I love St. Patrick's Day!

Printing Practice abc

Directions: Trace the *Cc*'s. Write your own.

NAME: _____

Directions: Match the sentences to the pictures.

1. I open gifts.

2. I see a clover.

3. I decorate a tree.

4. I see a pot of gold.

NAME: _____

Directions: Look for spelling. Circle the correct sentences.

Example: Christmas iss on December 25.
(Christmas is on December 25.)

1. St. Patrick's Day is March 17.

   St. Patrick's Daay is March 17.

2. People open gifts onn Christmas.

   People open gifts on Christmas.

3. People wear green on St. Patrick's Day.

   People wear green oon St. Patrick's Day.

Publishing

Christmas or St. Patrick's Day?

NAME: _____

Directions: Read the text. Draw a picture. Fill in the checklist.

> I like St. Patrick's Day. I like it because I get to wear green. I love St. Patrick's Day!

Checklist ☑

☐ Sentences begin with capital letters.

☐ Sentences end with punctuation.

☐ There are spaces between words.

NAME: _____

Directions: Circle the picture you like best. Write your opinion. Write a reason.

Valentine's Day	Halloween

Opinion

_____

I like _____.

Reason

_____

I like it because _____

_____.

Drafting

Valentine's Day or Halloween?

NAME: _____

Directions: Write about Valentine's Day or Halloween. Fill in the checklist.

Opinion _____

_ _

_____

(**Valentine's Day** or **Halloween**)

is the best holiday.

Reason   _____

_ _ _ _ _ _ _ _ _ _ _ _ _ _ _ _ _ _ _

I like it because _____

_ _

_____.

Closing _____

_ _

I love _____.

(**Valentine's Day** or **Halloween**)

Checklist ☑

❑ I state my opinion.

❑ I have a detail.

❑ I have a closing.

#51523—180 Days of Writing   © Shell Education

NAME: _____

Directions: Read the sentences. Draw pictures to match.

1. I see a jack-o-lantern.

2. I like hearts.

3. I see a witch.

Editing

Valentine's Day or Halloween?

NAME: _____

Directions: Choose the correct word. Write it.

Example: Valentine's Day _____ is _____
February 14.
(**is** or **iss**)

1. Halloween _____ be fun.
(**can** or **caan**)

2. People dress _____ costumes.
(**iin** or **in**)

3. People give cards _____ Valentine's Day.
(**onn** or **on**)

NAME: _____

Directions: Draw and write about Valentine's Day or Halloween. Fill in the checklist.

_____

- -

_____

_____

- -

_____

_____

- -

_____

Checklist

❑ Sentences begin with capital letters.

❑ Sentences end with punctuation.

❑ There are spaces between words.

NAME: _____

Directions: Circle the pictures about ocean animals.

fish

whale

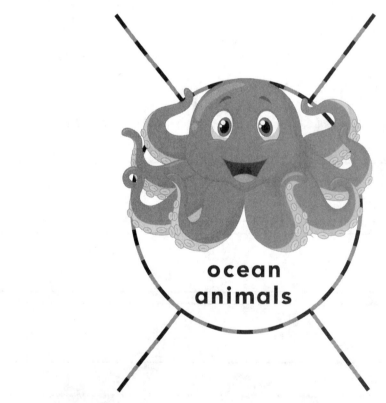

ocean animals

tiger

crab

NAME: _____

Directions: Read the text. Then, underline each sentence in green, red, or blue.

| **Green:** topic | **Red:** detail | **Blue:** closure |

Many animals live in the ocean. There are whales and sharks. There are lots of colorful fish. Ocean animals are very interesting.

Printing Practice abc

Directions: Trace the word. Write it on your own.

live _____

NAME: _____

Directions: Choose a word. Underline it.

Example: I (<u>see</u> or **saw**) a fish.

1. A crab lives in the (**sea** or **ocean**).

2. The ocean is (**big** or **large**).

3. There are (**many** or **few**) animals.

4. (**Whales** or **Sharks**) live in the ocean.

NAME: _____

Directions: Look for question marks. Circle the correct sentences.

Example: (Does a crab live in a shell?)
Does a crab live in a shell.

1. How big is a whale.

   How big is a whale?

2. Does an octopus have eight legs?

   Does an octopus have eight legs.

3. Do fish sleep behind rocks?

   Do fish sleep behind rocks.

NAME: _____

Directions: Read the text. Draw a picture. Fill in the checklist.

Many animals live in the ocean. There are whales and sharks. There are lots of colorful fish. Ocean animals are very interesting.

Checklist ☑

❑ Sentences begin with capital letters.

❑ Sentences end with punctuation.

❑ There are spaces between words.

NAME: _____

Directions: Trace the words about land animals.

elephant   horse

land animals

lion   bear

NAME: _____

Directions: Write about land animals. Fill in the checklist.

Topic

Land animals are _____

_____

_____.

Detail

_____

They _____

_____

_____.

Closing

_____

I _____ land animals.

Checklist ✔

❑ I have a topic sentence.

❑ I have a detail.

❑ I have a closing.

NAME: _____

Directions: Choose a word. Write it.

Example: A 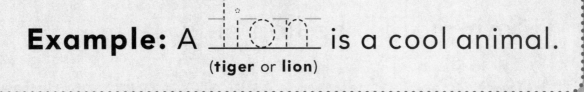 is a cool animal.
(**tiger** or **lion**)

_____
- -

1. An elephant is _____.

(**big** or **huge**)

_____
- -

2. I like _____.

(**horses** or **monkeys**)

_____
- -

3. A bear eats _____.

(**fish** or **food**)

NAME: _____

Directions: Add question marks to the sentences.

Example: Is the lion big<u>?</u>

1. Do you see the elephant

2. Is the tiger fast

3. Where are the horses

4. What does a bear eat

NAME: _____

Directions: Draw and write about land animals. Fill in the checklist.

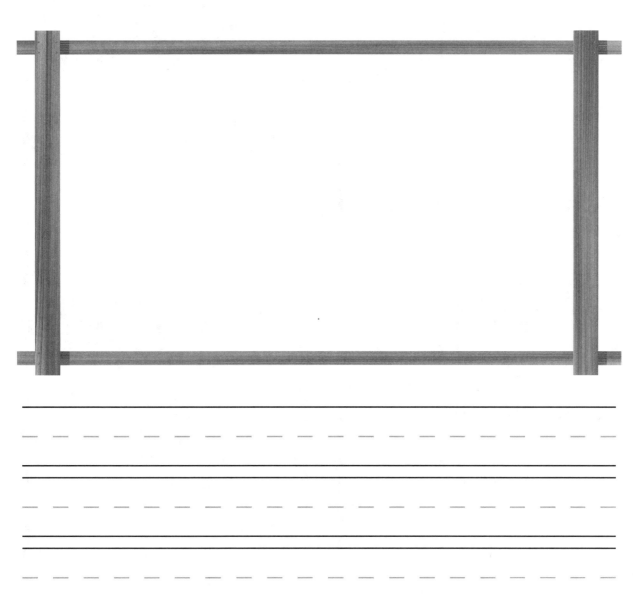

_____

_____

_____

_____

_____

Checklist ☑

❑ Sentences begin with capital letters.

❑ Sentences end with punctuation.

❑ There are spaces between words.

NAME: _____

Directions: Read the notes about being on a farm. Choose and underline one note in each box.

Who?

my uncle and I

my cousin and I

Where?

in Texas

in Montana

When?

on vacation

last week

Event 1

We walked around the farm.

We rode on a tractor.

Event 2

We fed the animals.

We ate a big dinner.

NAME: _____

Directions: Read the text. Then, underline each sentence in green, red, or blue.

| **Green:** introduction | **Red:** event | **Blue:** closure |

I went on vacation. I went to my uncle's farm. First, we rode on a tractor. Then, we ate a big dinner. It was lots of fun!

Printing Practice abc

Directions: Trace the word. Write it on your own.

has

NAME: _____

Directions: Look at the picture. Circle the details.

Directions: Draw your favorite detail from the picture.

NAME: _____

Directions: Look at the spelling. Circle the correct sentences.

Example: The pig kan oink.
(The pig can oink.)

1. A cow can give milk.

   A cow cna give milk.

2. Teh farmer rides a horse.

   The farmer rides a horse.

3. A duck quacks.

   A duc quacks.

Publishing Farms

NAME: _____

Directions: Read the text. Draw a picture. Fill in the checklist.

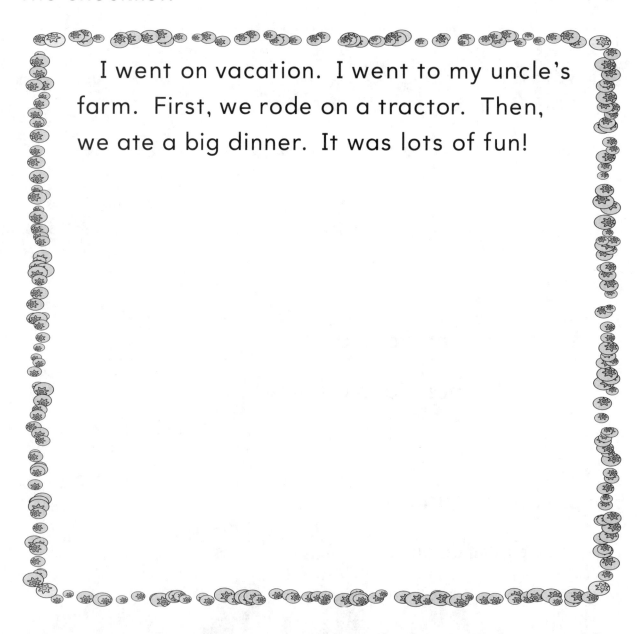

I went on vacation. I went to my uncle's farm. First, we rode on a tractor. Then, we ate a big dinner. It was lots of fun!

Checklist ☑

❏ Sentences begin with capital letters.

❏ Sentences end with punctuation.

❏ There are spaces between words.

NAME: _____

Directions: Imagine you visit a forest. Draw notes about the day.

Who?

Where?

When?

Event 1

Event 2

NAME: _____

Directions: Write about a forest. Fill in the checklist.

Drafting Forests

Introduction

I went to the forest with

_____

_____.

Events _____

First, _____.

Then, _____.

Closing Sentence

_____

_____

and I had so much fun!

Checklist ☑

❑ I have an introduction.

❑ I have events.

❑ I have a closing.

NAME: _____

Directions: Add details to the picture.

Editing | Forests

NAME: _____

Directions: Choose the correct word. Write it.

Example: _____We_____ visit the forest.
(**We** or **Wee**)

1. The forest _____ dark.
(**iss** or **is**)

2. _____ forest is big.
(**The** or **Teh**)

3. _____ we go to the forest?
(**Caan** or **Can**)

NAME: _____

Directions: Draw and write about a forest. Fill in the checklist.

Checklist ☑

❑ Sentences begin with capital letters.

❑ Sentences end with punctuation.

❑ There are spaces between words.

Prewriting   Soccer

NAME: _____

Directions: Read the notes about a soccer game. Choose and underline one note in each box.

Who?

my team and I

my family and I

Where?

at the park

on the field

When?

yesterday

Saturday

Event 1

I kicked the ball.

I ran around.

Event 2

I scored a goal.

I passed the ball.

Drafting

Soccer

NAME: _____

Directions: Read the text. Then, underline each sentence in green, red, or blue.

Green: introduction

Red: event

Blue: closure

I had a soccer game on Saturday. First, I kicked the ball. Then, I scored a goal. The team had a great game!

Printing Practice abc

Directions: Trace the *Ii*'s. Write your own.

I i   I i _____

NAME: _____

Directions: Look at the picture. Circle the details.

Directions: Draw your favorite detail from the picture.

NAME: _____

Directions: Look for capital letters. Circle the correct sentences.

Example: I went to the game with Jane.
I went to the game with jane.

1. al kicked the ball.

   Al kicked the ball.

2. Mia scored a goal.

   mia scored a goal.

3. Tim won an award.

   tim won an award.

NAME: _____

Directions: Read the text. Draw a picture. Fill in the checklist.

I had a soccer game on Saturday. First, I kicked the ball. Then, I scored a goal. The team had a great game!

Checklist ☑

❑ Sentences begin with capital letters.

❑ Sentences end with punctuation.

❑ There are spaces between words.

NAME: _____

Directions: Think about a baseball game.
Draw notes about it.

Who?

Where?

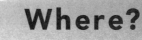

When?

Event 1

Event 2

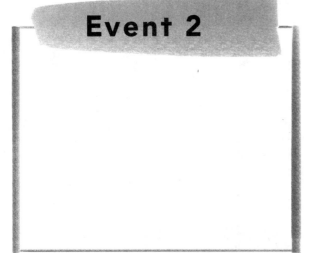

NAME: _____

Directions: Write about a baseball game. Fill in the checklist.

Introduction

I went to a baseball game with

_____

_____.

Events

_____

First, _____.

Then, _____.

Closing Sentence

_____

_____

and I had a great day!

Checklist ☑

❑ I have an introduction.

❑ I have events.

❑ I have a closing.

NAME: _____

Directions: Add details to the picture.

Editing | Baseball

NAME: _____

Directions: Choose the correct word. Write it.

Example: _____ ran to the base.
(**I** or **i**)

1. _____ play baseball with Nick.
   (**We** or **we**)

2. _____ hit the ball.
   (**I** or **i**)

3. _____ team won!
   (**our** or **Our**)

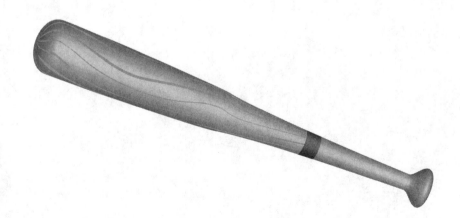

#51523—180 Days of Writing © Shell Education

NAME: _____

Directions: Draw and write about a baseball game. Fill in the checklist.

_____

_ _

_____

_ _

_____

_ _

_____

Checklist ☑

❏ Sentences begin with capital letters.

❏ Sentences end with punctuation.

❏ There are spaces between words.

Prewriting | Family

NAME: _____

Directions: Read the notes about spending a day with your family. Choose and underline one note in each box.

Who?

my cousins and I

my parents and I

Where?

at the movies

at the park

When?

last week

yesterday

Event 1

We bought snacks.

We played on the playground.

Event 2

We ate lunch.

We watched a movie.

#51523—180 Days of Writing   © Shell Education

NAME: _____

Directions: Read the text. Then, underline each sentence in green, red, or blue.

Green:
introduction

Red:
event

Blue:
closure

Last week, my cousins and I went to the movies. First, we got popcorn and candy. Then, we watched a funny movie. We had a great time!

Printing Practice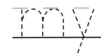

Directions: Trace the word. Write it on your own.

my

NAME: _____

Directions: Look at the picture. Circle the details.

Directions: Draw your favorite detail from the picture.

NAME: _____

Directions: Look for periods. Circle the correct sentences.

Editing

Family

> **Example:** (My family eats dinner.)
> My family eats dinner

1. My family plays games

   My family plays games.

2. My family has fun.

   My family has fun

3. We go to the park.

   We go to the park

Publishing

Family

NAME: _____

Directions: Read the text. Draw a picture. Fill in the checklist.

Last week, my cousins and I went to the movies. First, we got popcorn and candy. Then, we watched a funny movie. We had a great time!

Checklist ☑

❑ Sentences begin with capital letters.

❑ Sentences end with punctuation.

❑ There are spaces between words.

Prewriting
Friends

NAME: _____

Directions: Think about a time you did something with your friends. Draw notes about the day.

Who?

Where?

When?

Event 1

Event 2

NAME: _____

Drafting | Friends

Directions: Write about a day with your friends. Fill in the checklist.

Introduction

I spent a day with

_____

_____ .

Events _____

First, _____ .

Then, _____ .

Closing Sentence

_____

_____

and I had a great day!

Checklist ☑

☐ I have an introduction.

☐ I have events.

☐ I have a closing.

NAME: _____

Directions: Add details to the picture.

NAME: _____

Directions: Add periods to the sentences.

Example: Matt shares the blocks with Paul.

1. He listens to Bill

2. Kevin and Cole are helping

3. Tara and Ben are friends

4. I play with Maria

NAME: _____

Directions: Draw and write about your friend(s). Fill in the checklist.

_____

- -

_____

_____

- -

_____

_____

- -

_____

Checklist ☑

❑ Sentences begin with capital letters.

❑ Sentences end with punctuation.

❑ There are spaces between words.

NAME: _____

Directions: Circle the picture you like best.

Opinion: I like . . .

hamsters   **bunnies**

Directions: Place a check mark next to a reason.

Reasons

_____ They run on wheels.   _____ They eat veggies.

_____ They climb on arms.   _____ They hop.

NAME: _____

Directions: Read the text. Then, underline each sentence in green, red, or blue.

| **Green:** opinion | **Red:** detail | **Blue:** closure |

I like hamsters more than bunnies. I like them because they are small and cute. Hamsters make the best pets!

Printing Practice abc

Directions: Trace the word. Write it on your own.

like

NAME: _____

Directions: Match the sentences to the pictures.

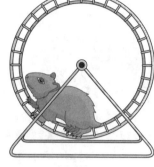

1. Bunnies are cute.

2. Hamsters run on wheels.

3. Bunnies eat carrots.

4. Hamsters eat corn.

NAME: _____

Directions: Look for capital letters. Circle the correct sentences.

Example: my hamster crawls on my arm.
(My hamster crawls on my arm.)

1. A bunny likes to hop.

   a bunny likes to hop.

2. Hamsters like to cuddle.

   hamsters like to cuddle.

3. i see a hamster run.

   I see a hamster run.

NAME: _____

Directions: Read the text. Draw a picture. Fill in the checklist.

I like hamsters more than bunnies. I like them because they are small and cute. Hamsters make the best pets!

Checklist ☑

❑ Sentences begin with capital letters.

❑ Sentences end with punctuation.

❑ There are spaces between words.

NAME: _____

Directions: Circle the picture you like best. Write your opinion. Write a reason.

dog   cat

Opinion

_____

I like _____.

Reason

_____

I like it because _____

_____

_____.

Drafting

Pet Dogs or Cats?

NAME: _____

Directions: Write about a dog or a cat. Fill in the checklist.

Opinion

_____

_____ is the best pet.

(**A dog** or **A cat**)

Reason

_____

I like it because _____

_____

_____.

Closing

_____

I love _____.

(**dogs** or **cats**)

Checklist ☑

❑ I state my opinion.

❑ I have a detail.

❑ I have a closing.

#51523—180 Days of Writing

NAME: _____

Directions: Read the sentences. Draw pictures to match.

1. Dogs like to bark.

2. A cat is furry.

3. A cat likes to purr.

NAME: _____

Directions: Choose the correct word. Write it.

Example: _Some_ dogs are fluffy.
(**Some** or **some**)

1. _____ cat meows.
(**a** or **A**)

2. _____ dog barks.
(**The** or **the**)

3. _____ cats are black.
(**Some** or **some**)

NAME: _____

Directions: Draw and write about a cat or a dog. Fill in the checklist.

Checklist ☑

❑ Sentences begin with capital letters.

❑ Sentences end with punctuation.

❑ There are spaces between words.

NAME: _____

Directions: Read the notes about your birthday. Choose and underline one note in each box.

Who?

my family and I

my friends and I

Where?

at the park

at home

When?

my fifth birthday

my sixth birthday

Event 1

I hit the piñata.

I opened presents.

Event 2

We ate cake.

We played a game.

NAME: _____

Directions: Read the text. Then, underline each sentence in green, red, or blue.

Green: introduction **Red:** event **Blue:** closure

On my sixth birthday, we went to the park. First, we played games. Then, we ate cake. It was my favorite birthday.

Printing Practice abc

Directions: Trace the word. Write it on your own.

was

NAME: _____

Directions: Look at the picture. Circle the details.

Directions: Draw your favorite detail from the picture.

#51523—180 Days of Writing   © Shell Education

NAME: _____

Directions: Look for capital letters. Circle the correct sentences.

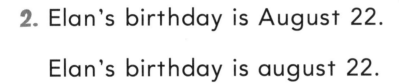

Example: Tess's birthday is october 14.
(Tess's birthday is October 14.)

1. Her birthday is july 9.

   Her birthday is July 9.

2. Elan's birthday is August 22.

   Elan's birthday is august 22.

3. His birthday is may 29.

   His birthday is May 29.

NAME: _____

Directions: Read the text. Draw a picture. Fill in the checklist.

On my sixth birthday, we went to the park. First, we played games. Then, we ate cake. It was my favorite birthday.

Checklist ☑

❑ Sentences begin with capital letters.

❑ Sentences end with punctuation.

❑ There are spaces between words.

NAME: _____

Directions: Think about a time you went to a birthday party. Draw notes about the day.

Who?

Where?

When?

Event 1

Event 2

Drafting

Favorite Birthday Party

NAME: _____

Directions: Write about a birthday party. Fill in the checklist.

Introduction

I went to a birthday party for _____

_____ .

Events _____

First, _____ .

Then, _____ .

Closing Sentence _____

_____

had a great birthday!

Checklist ☑

❑ I have an introduction.

❑ I have events.

❑ I have a closing.

NAME: _____

Directions: Add details to the picture.

NAME: _____

Directions: Choose the correct word. Write it.

Example

Johnny's birthday is in 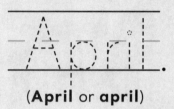.

(**April** or **april**)

_____

1. Maria's birthday is in _____.

(**may** or **May**)

_____

2. Kim's birthday is in _____.

(**July** or **july**)

_____

3. Jin's birthday is in _____.

(**june** or **June**)

NAME: _____

Directions: Draw and write about your favorite birthday party. Fill in the checklist.

_____
_ _ _ _ _ _ _ _ _ _ _ _ _ _ _ _ _ _
_____
_____
_ _ _ _ _ _ _ _ _ _ _ _ _ _ _ _ _ _
_____
_____
_ _ _ _ _ _ _ _ _ _ _ _ _ _ _ _ _ _
_____

Checklist ✔

❑ Sentences begin with capital letters.

❑ Sentences end with punctuation.

❑ There are spaces between words.

NAME: _____

Directions: Circle the picture you like best.

Opinion: I like . . .

apples	oranges

Directions: Place a check mark next to a reason.

Reasons

_____ They have stems.

_____ They are peeled.

_____ They are red or green.

_____ They are orange.

NAME: _____

Directions: Read the text. Then, underline each sentence in green, red, or blue.

> **Green:**   **Red:**   **Blue:**
> opinion   detail   closure

I like apples more than oranges. I like them because they are crunchy and sweet. Apples are yummy!

Printing Practice 🔤

Directions: Trace the word. Write it on your own.

NAME: _____

Directions: Match the sentences to the pictures.

1. An apple has a leaf.

2. Oranges are juicy.

3. You can slice an apple.

4. You can peel an orange.

NAME: _____

Directions: Look for periods. Circle the correct sentences.

> **Example:** (Apples are crunchy.)
> Apples are crunchy

1. Oranges are juicy.

   Oranges are juicy

2. Apples are red

   Apples are red.

3. Oranges have peels.

   Oranges have peels

Publishing

Apples or Oranges?

NAME: _____

Directions: Read the text. Draw a picture. Fill in the checklist.

I like apples more than oranges. I like them because they are crunchy and sweet. Apples are yummy!

Checklist ☑

❑ Sentences begin with capital letters.

❑ Sentences end with punctuation.

❑ There are spaces between words.

NAME: _____

Directions: Circle the picture you like best.
Write your opinion. Write a reason.

ice cream   cookies

Opinion

_____

I like _____.

Reason

_____

I like it/them because _____

_____.

Drafting
Ice Cream or Cookies?

NAME: _____

Directions: Write about ice cream or cookies. Fill in the checklist.

Opinion _____

_____

(Ice cream or **Cookies)**

is/are the best.

Reason _____

I like it/them because _____

_____

_____.

Closing _____

I love _____.

(ice cream or **cookies)**

Checklist ☑

❑ I state my opinion.

❑ I have a detail.

❑ I have a closing.

NAME: _____

Directions: Read the sentences. Draw pictures to match.

1. I like ice cream cones.

2. Ice cream melts on hot days.

3. Cookies are baked in ovens.

NAME: _____

Directions: Add periods to the sentences.

Example: I like the taste of cookies .

1. I like cookies because they are round

2. I like ice cream because it is creamy

3. I like cookies because they are warm

4. I like cookies more than ice cream

   #51523—180 Days of Writing

NAME: _____

Directions: Draw and write about ice cream or cookies. Fill in the checklist.

_____

_____

_____

_____

Checklist ☑

❑ Sentences begin with capital letters.

❑ Sentences end with punctuation.

❑ There are spaces between words.

NAME: _____

Directions: Circle the pictures about peacocks.

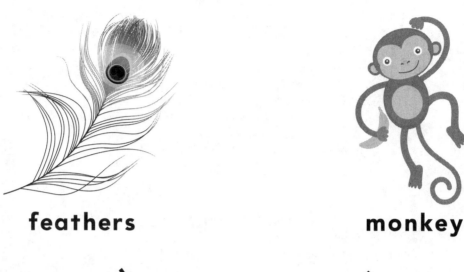

feathers　　　　　　**monkey**

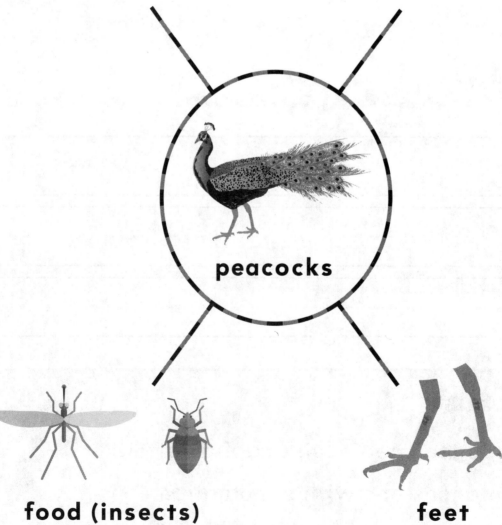

peacocks

food (insects)　　　　　　**feet**

NAME: _____

Directions: Read the text. Then, underline each sentence in green, red, or blue.

Green: topic   **Red:** detail   **Blue:** closure

Peacocks are a type of bird. They have colorful feathers. They eat insects. Peacocks are interesting.

Printing Practice abc

Directions: Trace the word. Write it on your own.

have

NAME: _____

Directions: Choose a word. Underline it.

Example: Birds have (<u>**beaks**</u> or **eyes**).

1. Birds have two wings and two (**legs** or **eyes**).

2. Birds have wings to (**fly** or **roam**).

3. Birds' legs let them (**walk** or **run**).

4. Birds (**have** or **lay**) eggs.

NAME: _____

Directions: Look for spelling. Circle the correct sentences.

> **Example:** Peacocks hav feathers.
> (Peacocks have feathers.)

1. Birds do nt have teeth.

   Birds do not have teeth.

2. Birds hatch frm eggs.

   Birds hatch from eggs.

3. Cardinals are red.

   Cardinals are rd.

4. Birds have two feet.

   Birds have two fet.

NAME: _____

Directions: Read the text. Draw a picture. Fill in the checklist.

Peacocks are a type of bird. They have colorful feathers. They eat insects. Peacocks are interesting.

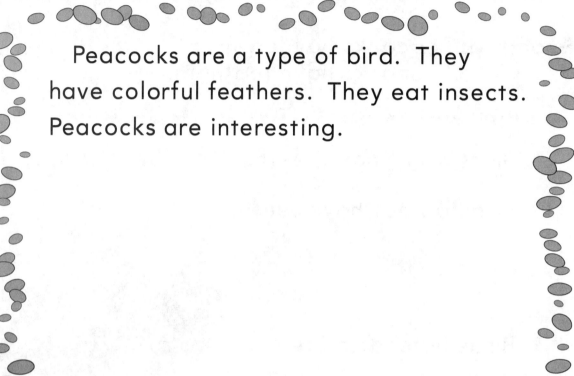

Checklist ☑

❑ Sentences begin with capital letters.

❑ Sentences end with punctuation.

❑ There are spaces between words.

    #51523—180 Days of Writing

NAME: _____

Directions: Trace the words about ducks.

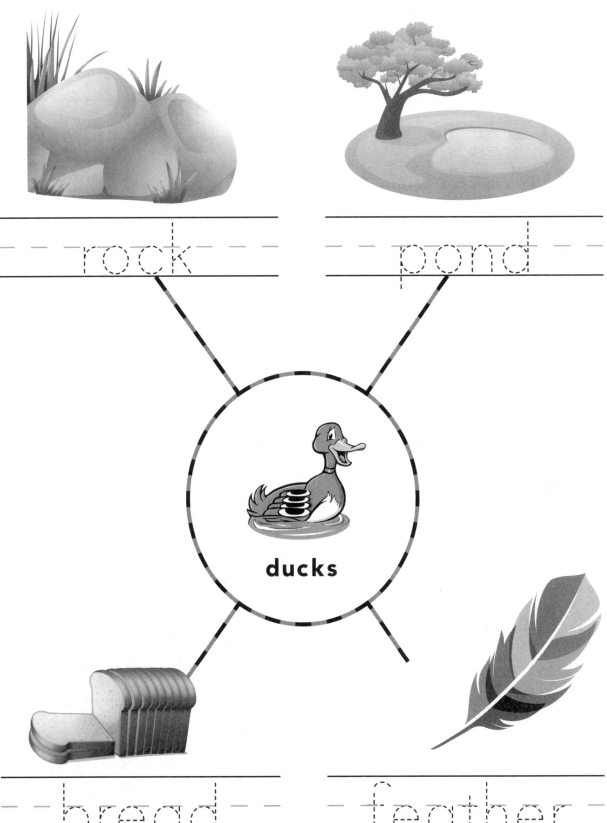

rock

pond

ducks

bread

feather

NAME: _____

Directions: Write about ducks. Fill in the checklist.

Topic
_____

Ducks are _____.

Detail
_____

They _____

_____.

Closing
_____

I love _____.

Checklist ☑

❏ I have a topic sentence.

❏ I have a detail.

❏ I have a closing.

#51523—180 Days of Writing

NAME: _____

Directions: Choose a word. Write it.

Example: Ducks eat ___bread___.
(**bread** or **food**)

Revising

Ducks

1. Ducks are _____ birds.
(**small** or **large**)

2. They _____ in the water.
(**swim** or **dive**)

3. They build _____.
(**nests** or **homes**)

4. They like to _____.
(**fly** or **quack**)

Editing | Ducks

NAME: _____

Directions: Choose the correct word. Write it.

Example: Ducks ___live___ near water.
(**live** or **liv**)

1. Ducks _____ in the water.
(**swm** or **swim**)

2. Ducks _____ bread.
(**eat** or **eet**)

3. They lay eggs in _____.
(**nests** or **nestz**)

4. They _____ to dive.
(**lke** or **like**)

NAME: _____

Directions: Draw and write about ducks. Fill in the checklist.

_____

_____

_____

_____

Checklist ☑

❑ Sentences begin with capital letters.

❑ Sentences end with punctuation.

❑ There are spaces between words.

NAME: _____

Directions: Circle the picture you like best.

Opinion: I like . . .

hot weather   cold weather

Directions: Place a check mark next to a reason.

Reasons

____ I play in the snow.   ____ I play in the sun.

____ I go swimming.   ____ I wear a coat.

NAME: _____

Directions: Read the text. Then, underline each sentence in green, red, or blue.

| **Green:** | **Red:** | **Blue:** |
| opinion | detail | closure |

I like hot weather the most. I like it because I get to go swimming in the pool. Hot weather is great!

Printing Practice abc

Directions: Trace the word. Write it on your own.

hot

NAME: _____

Directions: Match the sentences to the pictures.

1. I eat ice cream.

2. I drink hot chocolate.

3. I swim in hot weather.

4. I wear a jacket in cold weather.

NAME: _____

Directions: Look for capital letters. Circle the correct sentences.

Example: (The sun is shining.)
the sun is shining.

1. the clouds are in the sky.

   The clouds are in the sky.

2. The girl puts on her coat.

   the girl puts on her coat.

3. I see the sun outside.

   i see the sun outside.

NAME: _____

Directions: Read the text. Draw a picture. Fill in the checklist.

I like hot weather the most. I like it because I get to go swimming in the pool. Hot weather is great!

Checklist ☑

❑ Sentences begin with capital letters.

❑ Sentences end with punctuation.

❑ There are spaces between words.

NAME: _____

Directions: Circle the picture you like best. Write your opinion. Write a reason.

wind　　　　　　　**rain**

Opinion

_____

I like _____.

Reason

_____

I like it because _____

_____.

Drafting
Wind or Rain?

NAME: _____

Directions: Write about wind or rain. Fill in the checklist.

Opinion _____

_____ is the best.
(**Wind** or **Rain**)

Reason

_____
I like it because _____
_____
_____.

Closing _____

I love _____.
(**rain** or **wind**)

Checklist ☑

❑ I state my opinion.

❑ I have a detail.

❑ I have a closing.

NAME: _____

Directions: Read the sentences. Draw pictures to match.

1. I jump in puddles.

2. I fly a kite.

3. I use an umbrella.

NAME: _____

Directions: Choose the correct word. Write it.

Example: ___The___ rain hits the ground.
(The or **the)**

1. _____ flies her kite.
(**tia** or **Tia**)

2. _____ uses his umbrella.
(**Ethan** or **ethan**)

3. _____ loves the rain.
(**Lan** or **lan**)

#51523—180 Days of Writing   © Shell Education

NAME: _____

Directions: Draw and write about wind or rain.
Fill in the checklist.

_____
- -
_____
_____
- -
_____
_____
- -
_____

Checklist ✔

❑ Sentences begin with capital letters.

❑ Sentences end with punctuation.

❑ There are spaces between words.

NAME: _____

Directions: Circle the pictures about peanut butter and jelly sandwiches.

jelly

bread

Making a Peanut Butter and Jelly Sandwich

peanut butter

butter knife

NAME: _____

Directions: Read the text. Then, underline each sentence in green, red, or blue.

Green: topic   **Red:** detail   **Blue:** closure

It is easy to make a peanut butter and jelly sandwich. First, spread the peanut butter and jelly on the bread. Then, put the slices of bread together. Finally, you get to eat it!

Printing Practice abc

Directions: Trace the word. Write it on your own.

make _____

NAME: _____

Directions: Choose a word. Underline it.

Example: (<u>**Then**</u> or **Next**) get the bread.

1. (**Then** or **Next**), get out the jelly.

2. (**Now** or **Then**), get out the bread.

3. (**Next** or **Now**), put the peanut butter on the bread.

4. (**Then** or **Next**), put the jelly on the bread.

5. (**Now** or **Next**), put the slices of bread together.

NAME: _____

Directions: Look for periods. Circle the correct sentences.

Example: First, get out some jelly.
First, get out some jelly

---

1. Second, get out some peanut butter.

   Second, get out some peanut butter

2. Next, get out some bread

   Next, get out some bread.

3. Last, put the two slices of bread together.

   Last, put the two slices of bread together

NAME: _____

Directions: Read the text. Draw a picture. Fill in the checklist.

It is easy to make a peanut butter and jelly sandwich. First, spread the peanut butter and jelly on the bread. Then, put the slices of bread together. Finally, you get to eat it!

Checklist ☑

- ❑ Sentences begin with capital letters.
- ❑ Sentences end with punctuation.
- ❑ There are spaces between words.

#51523—180 Days of Writing

NAME: _____

Directions: Trace the words about washing your hands.

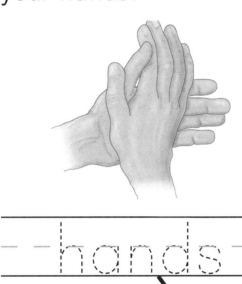

‑‑‑‑‑‑hands‑‑‑‑‑

‑‑‑‑‑water‑‑‑‑‑

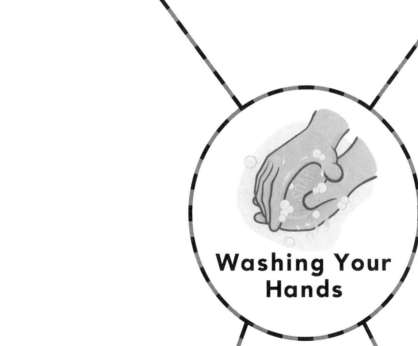

Washing Your Hands

soap

towel

Drafting

How to Wash Your Hands

NAME: _____

Directions: Write about washing your hands. Fill in the checklist.

Topic

Washing your hands is _____

_____

_____.

Detail

_____

You must _____

_____

_____.

Closing

_____

Make sure you _____.

Checklist ☑

❑ I have a topic sentence.

❑ I have a detail.

❑ I have a closing.

#51523—180 Days of Writing

© Shell Education

NAME: _____

Directions: Choose a word. Write it.

Example: <u>First</u> walk to the sink.
(**First** or **Now**)

_____

1. _____, turn on the water.
(**Now** or **First**)

_____

2. _____, put soap on your hands.
(**Then** or **Next**)

_____

3. _____, wash your hands.
(**Next** or **Now**)

_____

4. _____, dry your hands.
(**Last** or **Finally**)

NAME: _____

Directions: Add periods to the sentences.

Example: First, turn on the water .

1. Next, get soap on your hands

2. After that, wash your hands

3. Finally, dry your hands

4. Your hands are now clean

NAME: _____

Directions: Draw and write about washing your hands. Fill in the checklist.

_____
- - - - - - - - - - - - - - - - - -
_____
_____
- - - - - - - - - - - - - - - - - -
_____
_____
- - - - - - - - - - - - - - - - - -
_____

Checklist ☑

❏ Sentences begin with capital letters.

❏ Sentences end with punctuation.

❏ There are spaces between words.

ANSWER KEY

The activity pages that do not have specific answers to them are not included in this answer key. Students' answers will vary on these activity pages, so check that students are staying on task.

Week 1: Playing at the Park

Day 2 (page 15)

Introduction: I went to the park on Sunday with my sister.

Events: First, we played on the swings. Then, we went down the slide.

Closure: We had a great day.

Day 3 (page 16)

Students may circle the children playing, the flowers, the playground equipment, or any of the scenery.

Day 4 (page 17)
1. Al goes down the slide.
2. Liz plays in the sand.
3. She runs to the swings.
4. I am on the seesaw.

Week 2: Picnic at the Park

Day 3 (page 21)

Students may add food items or any other detail to the scenery.

Day 4 (page 22)
1. Nic sits on a blanket.
2. She eats a roll.
3. I look in the basket.
4. The park is fun.

Day 5 (page 23)

See Narrative Writing Rubric on page 201.

Week 3: What We Do in School

Day 2 (page 25)

Introduction: Today, I went to school.

Events: First, we did school work. Then, we went to recess.

Closure: I had a lot of fun at school.

Day 3 (page 26)

Students may circle the students or any of the details in the classroom.

Day 4 (page 27)
1. I read a story.
2. He eats lunch.
3. Luz plays at recess.
4. We do a puzzle.

Week 4: School Rules

Day 3 (page 31)

Students may draw students or items that belong in a classroom.

Day 4 (page 32)
1. Zan raises **his hand**.
2. **He is** a good listener.
3. She shares **her toys**.

Day 5 (page 33)

See Narrative Writing Rubric on page 201.

Week 5: Spring or Fall?

Day 2 (page 35)

Opinion: I like spring more than fall.

Details: I like it because there are lots of fun things I can do.

Closure: Spring is the best season.

Day 3 (page 36)
1. He likes the pumpkin.
2. I plant flowers.
3. She bounces a ball.
4. The sun is bright.
5. I see a leaf.

Day 4 (page 37)
1. It is raining.
2. Here is a pumpkin.
3. The flower is pink.
4. I like the rain.

Week 6: Summer or Winter?

Day 4 (page 42)
1. I like to swim.
2. The bear sleeps.
3. They play in snow.
4. I go to the beach.
5. I wear a coat.

Day 5 (page 43)

See Opinion Writing Rubric on page 199.

Week 7: Sight and Smell

Day 1 (page 44)

Students may circle all of the items except the ear.

Day 2 (page 45)

Topic: We have five senses.

Details: We use our eyes to see. We use our noses to smell.

Closure: It is great to have senses!

Day 4 (page 47)
1. She smells pizza.
2. I see flowers.
3. They smell muffins.

Week 8: Taste and Touch

Day 1 (page 49)

Students may trace all of the items.

Day 4 (page 52)
1. **I** taste the apple.
2. **He** feels the crayon.
3. **She** feels a horse.
4. **I** eat cookies.

Day 5 (page 53)

See Informative/Explanatory Writing Rubric on page 200.

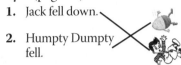

ANSWER KEY (cont.)

Week 9: Firefighters

Day 1 (page 54)

Students may circle the following: helmet, hose, and truck.

Day 2 (page 55)

Topic: Firefighters help the community.

Details: They keep people safe. They stop fires.

Closure: Firefighters are heroes.

Day 4 (page 57)

1. Firefighters rescue people.
2. Firefighters use ladders.
3. Firefighters work at fire stations.

Week 10: Police Officers

Day 1 (page 59)

Students may trace the following: car, hat, and badge.

Day 4 (page 62)

1. Police officers wear badges**.**
2. They drive in cars with sirens**.**
3. Police officers wear uniforms**.**
4. Police officers work very hard**.**
5. Police officers are heroes**.**

Day 5 (page 63)

See Informative/Explanatory Writing Rubric on page 200.

Week 11: Humpty Dumpty or Jack and Jill

Day 2 (page 65)

Opinion: I like "Jack and Jill" more than "Humpty Dumpty."

Details: I like it because it is funny.

Closure: "Jack and Jill" is my favorite.

Day 3 (page 66)

1. Jack fell down.
2. Humpty Dumpty fell.
3. Jill had a pail.
4. Jack and Jill went up a hill.

Day 4 (page 67)

1. Jack fell down.
2. And Jill came tumbling after.
3. Jack and Jill were both okay.

Week 12: Itsy Bitsy Spider or Little Bo Peep

Day 4 (page 72)

1. The sheep **are lost**.
2. The spider climbs **a web**.
3. I see **a sheep**.
4. **I see** the spider.

Day 5 (page 73)

See Opinion Writing Rubric on page 199.

Week 13: Sun and Moon

Day 1 (page 74)

Students may circle the following: hot, half moon, and crescent moon.

Day 2 (page 75)

Topic: The sun and the moon are in the sky.

Details: The sun comes out in the day. The moon comes out at night.

Closure: They are both important to Earth.

Day 4 (page 77)

1. The sun is bright.
2. The moon is smaller than Earth.
3. The sun is hot.

Week 14: Earth

Day 1 (page 79)

Students may trace all of the items.

Day 4 (page 82)

1. **The** planets go around the sun.
2. **There** are eight planets.
3. **The** planet Earth is mostly water.

Day 5 (page 83)

See Informative/Explanatory Writing Rubric on page 200.

Week 15: Christmas or St. Patrick's Day

Day 2 (page 85)

Opinion: I like St. Patrick's Day.

Details: I like it because I get to wear green.

Closure: I love St. Patrick's Day!

Day 3 (page 86)

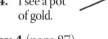

1. I open gifts.
2. I see a clover.
3. I decorate a tree.
4. I see a pot of gold.

Day 4 (page 87)

1. St. Patrick's Day is March 17.
2. People open gifts on Christmas.
3. People wear green on St. Patrick's Day.

ANSWER KEY *(cont.)*

Week 16: Valentine's Day or Halloween

Day 4 (page 92)
1. Halloween **can** be fun.
2. People dress **in** costumes.
3. People give cards **on** Valentine's Day.

Day 5 (page 93)
See Opinion Writing Rubric on page 199.

Week 17: Ocean Animals

Day 1 (page 94)
Students may circle the following: fish, whale, and crab.

Day 2 (page 95)
Topic: Many animals live in the ocean.
Details: There are whales and sharks. There are lots of colorful fish.
Closure: Ocean animals are very interesting.

Day 4 (page 97)
1. How big is a whale?
2. Does an octopus have eight legs?
3. Do fish sleep behind rocks?

Week 18: Land Animals

Day 1 (page 99)
Students may trace all of the words.

Day 4 (page 102)
1. Do you see the elephant?
2. Is the tiger fast?
3. Where are the horses?
4. What does a bear eat?

Day 5 (page 103)
See Informative/Explanatory Writing Rubric on page 200.

Week 19: Farms

Day 2 (page 105)
Introduction: I went on vacation. I went to my uncle's farm.
Events: First, we rode on a tractor. Then, we ate a big dinner.
Closure: It was lots of fun!

Day 3 (page 106)
Students may circle the animals or any of the scenery on the farm.

Day 4 (page 107)
1. A cow can give milk.
2. The farmer rides a horse.
3. A duck quacks.

Week 20: Forests

Day 3 (page 111)
Students may add animals and more trees to the picture.

Day 4 (page 112)
1. The forest **is** dark.
2. **The** forest is big.
3. **Can** we go to the forest?

Day 5 (page 113)
See Narrative Writing Rubric on page 201.

Week 21: Soccer

Day 2 (page 115)
Introduction: I had a soccer game on Saturday.
Events: First, I kicked the ball. Then, I scored a goal.
Closure: The team had a great game!

Day 3 (page 116)
Students may circle the soccer players or anything else on the soccer field.

Day 4 (page 117)
1. Al kicked the ball.
2. Mia scored a goal.
3. Tim won an award.

Week 22: Baseball

Day 3 (page 121)
Students may add players or a play in action on the baseball field.

Day 4 (page 122)
1. **We** play baseball with Nick.
2. **I** hit the ball.
3. **Our** team won!

Day 5 (page 123)
See Narrative Writing Rubric on page 201.

Week 23: Family

Day 2 (page 125)
Introduction: Last week, my cousins and I went to the movies.
Events: First, we got popcorn and candy. Then, we watched a funny movie.
Closure: We had a great time at the movies!

Day 3 (page 126)
Details may include any of the family members or any of the elements in the scenery.

Day 4 (page 127)
1. My family plays games.
2. My family has fun.
3. We go to the park.

Week 24: Friends

Day 3 (page 131)
Students may add more to the background scenery and draw themselves playing with friends.

Day 4 (page 132)
1. He listens to Bill.
2. Kevin and Cole are helping.
3. Tara and Ben are friends.
4. I play with Maria.

Day 5 (page 133)
See Narrative Writing Rubric on page 201.

ANSWER KEY *(cont.)*

Week 25: Pet Hamsters or Bunnies?

Day 2 (page 135)

Opinion: I like hamsters more than bunnies.

Details: I like them because they are small and cute.

Closiure: Hamsters make the best pets!

Day 3 (page 136)
1. Bunnies are cute.
2. Hamsters run on wheels.
3. Bunnies eat carrots.
4. Hamsters eat corn.

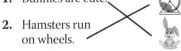

Day 4 (page 137)
1. A bunny likes to hop.
2. Hamsters like to cuddle.
3. I see a hamster run.

Week 26: Pet Dogs or Cats?

Day 4 (page 142)
1. **A** cat meows.
2. **The** dog barks.
3. **Some** cats are black.

Day 5 (page 143)

See Opinion Writing Rubric on page 199.

Week 27: My Birthday

Day 2 (page 145)

Introduction: On my sixth birthday, we went to the park.

Events: First, we played games. Then, we ate cake.

Closure: It was my favorite birthday.

Day 3 (page 146)

Details may include the balloons, the cake, the party hats or any element of the scene.

Day 4 (page 147)
1. Her birthday is July 9.
2. Elan's birthday is August 22.
3. His birthday is May 29.

Week 28: Favorite Birthday Party

Day 3 (page 151)

Students may add more decorations or more gifts to the picture.

Day 4 (page 152)
1. Maria's birthday is in **May**.
2. Kim's birthday is in **July**.
3. Jin's birthday is in **June**.

Day 5 (page 153)

See Narrative Writing Rubric on page 201.

Week 29: Apples or Oranges?

Day 2 (page 155)

Opinion: I like apples more than oranges.

Details: I like them because they are crunchy and sweet.

Closure: Apples are yummy!

Day 3 (page 156)
1. An apple has a leaf.
2. Oranges are juicy.
3. You can slice an apple.
4. You can peel an orange.

Day 4 (page 157)
1. Oranges are juicy.
2. Apples are red.
3. Oranges have peels.

Week 30: Ice Cream or Cookies?

Day 4 (page 162)
1. I like cookies because they are round.
2. I like ice cream because it is creamy.
3. I like cookies because they are warm.
4. I like cookies more than ice cream.

Day 5 (page 163)

See Opinion Writing Rubric on page 199.

Week 31: Peacocks

Day 1 (page 164)

Students may circle the following: feathers, food (insects), and feet.

Day 2 (page 165)

Topic: Peacocks are a type of bird.

Details: They have colorful feathers. They eat insects.

Closure: Peacocks are interesting.

Day 4 (page 167)
1. Birds do not have teeth.
2. Birds hatch from eggs.
3. Cardinals are red.
4. Birds have two feet.

Week 32: Ducks

Day 1 (page 169)

Students may trace all of the words.

Day 4 (page 172)
1. Ducks **swim** in the water.
2. Ducks **eat** bread.
3. They lay eggs in **nests**.
4. They **like** to dive.

Day 5 (page 173)

See Informative/Explanatory Writing Rubric on page 200.

ANSWER KEY *(cont.)*

Week 33: Hot or Cold?

Day 2 (page 175)

Opinion: I like hot weather the most.

Details: I like it because I get to go swimming in the pool.

Closure: Hot weather is great!

Day 3 (page 176)

1. I eat ice cream.
2. I drink hot chocolate.
3. I swim in hot weather.
4. I wear a jacket in cold weather.

Day 4 (page 177)

1. The clouds are in the sky.
2. The girl puts on her coat.
3. I see the sun outside.

Week 34: Wind or Rain?

Day 4 (page 182)

1. **Tia** flies her kite.
2. **Ethan** uses his umbrella.
3. **Lan** loves the rain.

Day 5 (page 183)

See Opinion Writing Rubric on page 199.

Week 35: How to Make a Peanut Butter and Jelly Sandwich

Day 1 (page 184)

Students may circle the following: jelly, bread, peanut butter, and butter knife.

Day 2 (page 185)

Topic: It is easy to make a peanut butter and jelly sandwich.

Details: First, spread the peanut butter and jelly on the bread. Then, put the slices of bread together.

Closure: Finally, you get to eat it!

Day 4 (page 187)

1. Second, get out some peanut butter.
2. Next, get out some bread.
3. Last, put the two slices of bread together.

Week 36: How to Wash Your Hands

Day 1 (page 189)

Students may trace all of the words.

Day 4 (page 192)

1. Next, get soap on your hands.
2. After that, wash your hands.
3. Finally, dry your hands.
4. Your hands are now clean.

Day 5 (page 193)

See Informative/Explanatory Writing Rubric on page 200.

OPINION WRITING RUBRIC

Directions: Evaluate students' work in each category by circling one number in each row. Students have opportunities to score up to five points in each row and up to 15 points total.

	Exceptional Writing	Quality Writing	Developing Writing
Focus and Organization	States a clear opinion. Includes lots of details. Includes a strong closing.	States an opinion. Includes at least one detail. Includes a closing.	States an unclear opinion. Includes few or unclear details. Does not include a closing.
Points	5 4	3 2	1 0
Written Expression	Uses varied and interesting descriptive words. Maintains a consistent voice and uses a tone that supports meaning.	Uses some descriptive words. Maintains a consistent voice.	Uses a limited or an unvaried vocabulary. Provides an inconsistent voice.
Points	5 4	3 2	1 0
Language Conventions	Sentences begin with capital letters. Sentences end in correct punctuation. Words in sentences have correct spacing between them.	Some sentences begin with capital letters. Some sentences end in correct punctuation. Most words in sentences have correct spacing between them.	Most sentences begin with lowercase letters. Sentences end in incorrect punctuation, or no punctuation is used. Words have incorrect spacing between them.
Points	5 4	3 2	1 0

Total Points: _____

INFORMATIVE/EXPLANATORY WRITING RUBRIC

Directions: Evaluate students' work in each category by circling one number in each row. Students have opportunities to score up to five points in each row and up to 15 points total.

	Exceptional Writing	Quality Writing	Developing Writing
Focus and Organization	States a clear topic sentence. Includes lots of details. Includes a strong closing.	States a topic sentence. Includes at least one detail. Includes a closing.	States an unclear topic sentence. Includes few or unclear details. Does not include a closing.
Points	5 4	3 2	1 0
Written Expression	Uses varied and interesting descriptive words. Maintains a consistent voice and uses a tone that supports meaning.	Uses some descriptive words. Maintains a consistent voice.	Uses a limited or an unvaried vocabulary. Provides an inconsistent voice.
Points	5 4	3 2	1 0
Language Conventions	Sentences begin with capital letters. Sentences end in correct punctuation. Words in sentences have correct spacing between them.	Some sentences begin with capital letters. Some sentences end in correct punctuation. Most words in sentences have correct spacing between them.	Most sentences begin with lowercase letters. Sentences end in incorrect punctuation, or no punctuation is used. Words have incorrect spacing between them.
Points	5 4	3 2	1 0

Total Points: _____

NARRATIVE WRITING RUBRIC

Directions: Evaluate students' work in each category by circling one number in each row. Students have opportunities to score up to five points in each row and up to 15 points total.

	Exceptional Writing	Quality Writing	Developing Writing
Focus and Organization	States a clear introduction. Includes lots of events. Includes a strong closing.	States an introduction. Includes at least one event. Includes a closing.	States an unclear introduction. Includes few or unclear events. Does not include a closing.
Points	5 4	3 2	1 0
Written Expression	Uses varied and interesting descriptive words. Maintains a consistent voice and uses a tone that supports meaning.	Uses some descriptive words. Maintains a consistent voice.	Uses a limited or an unvaried vocabulary. Provides an inconsistent voice.
Points	5 4	3 2	1 0
Language Conventions	Sentences begin with capital letters. Sentences end in correct punctuation. Words in sentences have correct spacing between them.	Some sentences begin with capital letters. Some sentences end in correct punctuation. Most words in sentences have correct spacing between them.	Most sentences begin with lowercase letters. Sentences end in incorrect punctuation, or no punctuation is used. Words have incorrect spacing between them.
Points	5 4	3 2	1 0

Total Points: _____

OPINION WRITING ANALYSIS

Directions: Record each student's rubric scores (page 199) in the appropriate columns. Add the totals every two weeks and record the sums in the Total Scores column. You can view: (1) which students are not understanding the opinion genre and (2) how students progress after multiple encounters with the opinion genre.

Student Name	Week 6	Week 12	Week 16	Week 26	Week 30	Week 34	Total Scores
Average Classroom Score							

INFORMATIVE/EXPLANATORY WRITING ANALYSIS

Directions: Record each student's rubric score (page 200) in the appropriate columns. Add the totals every two weeks and record the sums in the Total Scores column. You can view: (1) which students are not understanding the informative/explanatory genre and (2) how students progress after multiple encounters with the informative/explanatory genre.

Student Name	Week 8	Week 10	Week 14	Week 18	Week 32	Week 36	Total Scores
Average Classroom Score							

NARRATIVE WRITING ANALYSIS

Directions: Record each student's rubric score (page 201) in the appropriate columns. Add the totals every two weeks and record the sums in the Total Scores column. You can view: (1) which students are not understanding the narrative genre and (2) how students progress after multiple encounters with the narrative genre.

Student Name	Week 2	Week 4	Week 20	Week 22	Week 24	Week 28	Total Scores
Average Classroom Score							

THE WRITING PROCESS

STEP 1: PREWRITING

Think about the topic. Brainstorm ideas.

STEP 2: DRAFTING

Use your ideas to write a draft. Don't worry about errors.

STEP 3: REVISING

Read your draft. Think about the vocabulary. Think about the organization. Make changes to improve your writing.

STEP 4: EDITING

Reread your draft. Check for errors in spelling, punctuation, and grammar.

STEP 5: PUBLISHING

Create a final draft. Be sure to use your best printing.

EDITING MARKS

Editing Marks	Symbol Names	Example
=	capitalization symbol	<u>david</u> ate grapes.
/	lowercase symbol	My mother hugged Me.
⊙	insert period symbol	The clouds are in the sky⊙
sp ○	check spelling symbol	I (laffed) at the story.
∿	transpose symbol	How you are?
∧	insert symbol	Would you ∧please pass the pizza?
∧,	insert comma symbol	I have cats, dogs∧ and goldfish.
" " ∨ ∨	insert quotations symbol	∨That is amazing,∨ she shouted.
ℯ	deletion symbol	Will you call call me?
#	add space symbol	I run to#the tree.

OPINION WRITING TIPS

INFORMATIVE/EXPLANATORY WRITING TIPS

1. Choose a topic.

2. Write a strong topic sentence.

3. Write facts about the topic.

4. Finish with a strong statement about the topic.

5. Check for correct spelling and punctuation.

NARRATIVE WRITING TIPS

Write a topic sentence that tells what your story is about.

Write in a logical order with a beginning, a middle, and an end.

Include characters.

Join the sentences with the words *first*, *next*, *then*, and *finally*.

Use lots of details and sensory words.

Check for correct spelling and punctuation.

Opinion Writing

Informative/Explanatory Writing

Narrative Writing

PEER/SELF-EDITING CHECKLIST

Directions: Place a check mark in front of each item as you check it.

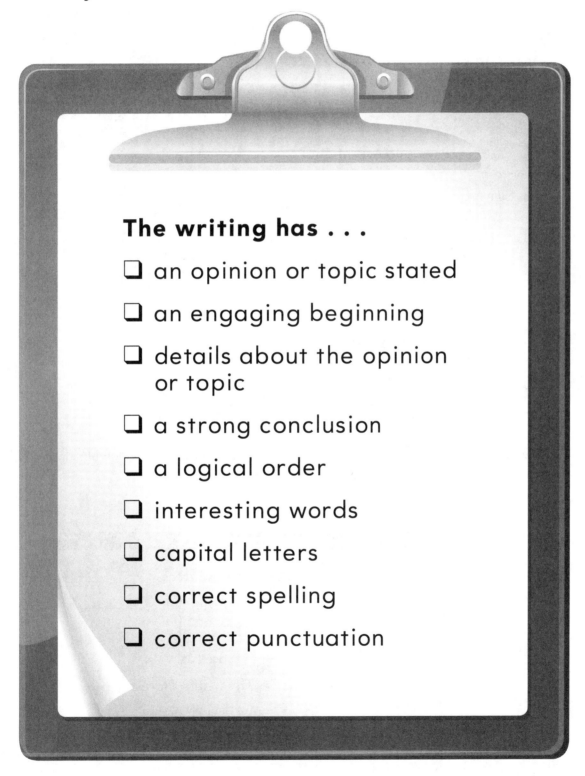

The writing has . . .

❑ an opinion or topic stated

❑ an engaging beginning

❑ details about the opinion or topic

❑ a strong conclusion

❑ a logical order

❑ interesting words

❑ capital letters

❑ correct spelling

❑ correct punctuation

DIGITAL RESOURCES

Accessing the Digital Resources

The digital resources can be downloaded by following these steps:

1. Go to **www.tcmpub.com/digital**

2. Sign in or create an account.

3. Click **Redeem Content** and enter the ISBN number, located on page 2 and the back cover, into the appropriate field on the website.

ISBN:
9781425815233

4. Respond to the prompts using the book to view your account and available digital content.

5. Choose the digital resources you would like to download. You can download all the files at once, or you can download a specific group of files.

Please note: Some files provided for download have large file sizes. Download times for these larger files will vary based on your download speed.

CONTENTS OF THE DIGITAL RESOURCES

Teacher Resources

- Informative/Explanatory Writing Analysis
- Narrative Writing Analysis
- Opinion Writing Analysis
- Writing Rubric
- Writing Signs

Student Resources

- Peer/Self-Editing Checklist
- Editing Marks
- Practice Pages
- The Writing Process
- Writing Prompts
- Writing Tips

NOTES

NOTES